The Creative Curriculum® *for* Preschool

Teaching Guide
Beginning the Year

Kai-leé Berke, Carol Aghayan, Cate Heroman

TeachingStrategies® · Bethesda, MD

Copyright © 2010, 2016 by Teaching Strategies, LLC.

All rights reserved. No part of this text may be reproduced in any form or by any electronic or mechanical means, including information storage and retrieval systems, without prior written permission from Teaching Strategies, LLC, except in the case of brief quotations embodied in critical articles or reviews.

An exception is also made for the forms and the letters to families that are included in this guide. Permission is granted to duplicate those pages for use by the teachers/providers of the particular program that purchased these materials in order to implement *The Creative Curriculum® for Preschool* in the program. These materials may not be duplicated for training purposes without the express written permission of Teaching Strategies, LLC.

The publisher and the authors cannot be held responsible for injury, mishap, or damages incurred during the use of or because of the information in this book. The authors recommend appropriate and reasonable supervision at all times based on the age and capability of each child.

English editing: Lydia Paddock, Jayne Lytel
Design and layout: Jeff Cross, Amy Jackson, Abner Nieves
Spanish translation: Claudia Caicedo Núñez
Spanish editing: Judith F. Wohlberg, Alicia Fontán
Cover design: Laura Monger Design
Cover galoshes photo: Courtesy of Community Playthings

Teaching Strategies, LLC.
4500 East West Highway, Suite 300
Bethesda, MD 20814

www.TeachingStrategies.com

978-1-60617-382-4

Library of Congress Cataloging-in-Publication Data

Berke, Kai-leé.
  The creative curriculum for preschool teaching guide : beginning the year
/ Kai-leé Berke, Carol Aghayan, Cate Heroman.
     p. cm.
  ISBN 978-1-60617-382-4
  1. Preschool teaching. 2. Readiness for school. I. Aghayan, Carol. II.
Heroman, Cate. III. Title.
  LB1140.3.B47 2010
  372.1102--dc22
                               2010002153

Teaching Strategies, Creative Curriculum, LearningGames, GOLD, GOLDplus, Mighty Minutes, and Mega Minutos names and logos are registered trademarks of Teaching Strategies, LLC, Bethesda, MD. Brand-name products of other companies are suggested only for illustrative purposes and are not required for implementation of the curriculum.

5 6 7 8 9 10 11 12   20 19 18 17 16
       Printing   Year Printed

Printed and bound in China

Table of Contents

Getting Started

- 2 Introduction
- 3 Preparing for the First Days of School
  - 4 Welcome Families to the Program
  - 5 Arrange the Physical Environment
  - 6 Plan Your Daily Schedule
  - 7 Plan for Each Time of Your Day
  - 9 Plan for Ongoing, Observation-Based Assessment
- 11 Preparing for Wow! Experiences

Focus Questions

- 14 What names do we need to know at school?
  (Days 1–5)
- 26 What should we do if we get sad or scared at school?
  (Days 1–3)
- 34 What are our rules?
  (Days 1–5)
- 46 When do things happen at school?
  (Days 1–3)
- 54 Who works at our school?
  (Days 1–4)
- 64 How do we make and keep friends?
  How can we be part of a group?
  (Days 1–5)

Ministudy

- 78 What sounds do we hear at school?
  Where do they come from?
  (Days 1–5)

Resources

- 92 Integrating Mathematics Throughout the Day
- 96 Integrating Literacy Throughout the Day
- 99 Children's Books
- 101 Teacher Resources
- 102 Weekly Planning Form

Getting Started

Introduction

The beginning of the school year is an exciting time! This *Teaching Guide* contains a collection of daily plans that will help you start it off right. During the first several weeks of the school year, you will be busy supporting children as they say good-bye to their families, become familiar with the classroom and school routines, and learn to find comfort in being a member of the classroom community while maintaining a secure connection to home.

Whether children are new to preschool or not, expect that many will experience strong emotions—fear, anxiety, extreme excitement, sadness, or frustration. Throughout this *Teaching Guide,* you'll find strategies for supporting children's social–emotional development as they become comfortable in their new environment. The time you invest now in building relationships with children and their families is well spent, and it will reward you with positive interactions throughout the year.

Children will have many questions as they navigate their new surroundings. We've chosen six that we consider typical and used them to structure your classroom conversations and learning during the first five weeks of school. For the last week, you'll find a collection of daily plans that you may use to conduct a ministudy with the children on the sounds they hear at school. During this weeklong study, you'll guide children through the process of generating questions they would like answered, investigating those questions, and celebrating their learning.

Preparing for the First Days of School

Planning carefully for the first few days of school can ease transitions and help children feel more comfortable and secure. If you can anticipate their needs, you'll be better prepared to plan for their arrival and support them successfully.

Some children with prior experience in group settings may have learned the skills needed to be members of a classroom community. For other children, preschool may be their first experience away from home or in a group.

In either case, expect that the children are wondering about what lies ahead. Read more about guidelines for planning for the first days of school in *The Creative Curriculum® for Preschool, Volume 1: The Foundation,* Chapter 4.

To help you prepare for the first days of school, this guide includes a checklist of reminders for you. Not all of them may apply to your particular situation. Add to the list as needed. Remember, time spent in planning and preparing for the first days of school will help make the early days smooth and ease children into the school environment.

Beginning the Year Getting Started

Welcome Families to the Program

- [ ] Obtain contact information from families.

- [ ] Review family and child records. Note information to make a meaningful connection at the initial meeting.

- [ ] Develop a plan for storing child and family information.

- [ ] Send a welcome letter to the child and the family. Letters to families can be customized to your program and are available via the *Classroom and Family Resources Online Portal*. The online portal is a password-protected URL that you will receive via e-mail.

- [ ] Post a picture of yourself, an assistant, and other individuals who will be responsible for caring for the children. Include a short summary about yourself.

- [ ] Review *The Creative Curriculum® for Preschool, Volume 1: The Foundation,* Chapter 5 for ideas on getting to know families and making families feel welcome in your program.

- [ ] Plan a system for ongoing communication with families, e.g., a daily message board, phone calls, or weekly emails. See *Volume 1: The Foundation,* Chapter 5 for ideas on communicating with families.

Beginning the Year Getting Started

Arrange the Physical Environment

☐ Refer to the following resources for setting up the physical environment:
  - "Setting Up a Classroom for 20 Preschool Children" found on the *Classroom and Family Resources Online Portal*.
  - *The Creative Curriculum® for Preschool, Volume 1: The Foundation*, Chapter 2
  - *The Creative Curriculum® for Preschool, Volume 2: Interest Areas*

☐ Sketch a floor plan and seek feedback from your coach, mentor, or colleagues.

☐ Arrange the basic furnishings in the classroom.

☐ Assess the classroom materials for items that need to be replaced or bought.

☐ Keep a prioritized wish list of materials you would like to order.

☐ Label classroom materials, referring to *The Creative Curriculum® for Preschool, Volume 1: The Foundation* and *Volume 2: Interest Areas* for guidance.

☐ Evaluate the current classroom materials available:
  - Remove any unusable materials, e.g., broken or missing items.
  - Organize materials by interest areas.
  - Select a limited number of materials for each interest area that would be most appropriate for the beginning of school, e.g., open-ended, familiar, limited supervision necessary.
  - Label and store remaining materials.

☐ Evaluate the materials to be sure that they relate directly to children's experiences and do not depict stereotypes. Consider the children's family backgrounds as you select materials and plan learning experiences.

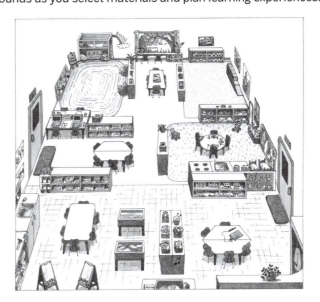

The Creative Curriculum® for Preschool

Beginning the Year Getting Started

Arrange the Physical Environment, continued

- [ ] Keep an eye open for "found" items to make the environment comfortable and attractive, such as items from nature.

- [ ] Review and apply the guidelines found in *The Creative Curriculum® for Preschool, Volume 1: The Foundation,* Chapter 2 for making your space comfortable and attractive.

- [ ] Make sure there is a place to store everything to avoid clutter.

Plan Your Daily Schedule

- [ ] Find out the school or center's schedule and get specific times for the following:
  - arrival and departure
  - meals and snacks
  - outdoors
  - nap or rest time
  - other factors that will impact the class schedule

- [ ] Review *The Creative Curriculum® for Preschool, Volume 1: The Foundation,* Chapter 2 and the appendix for a variety of schedules.

- [ ] Begin a rough draft of your daily schedule. Start with the "fixed" times, such as arrival, departure, lunch, and other events.

- [ ] Include times for large group, choice time, small group, read-aloud, and large-group roundup.

- [ ] Create your daily schedule using pictures and words. See the example in *The Creative Curriculum® for Preschool, Volume 1: The Foundation,* Chapter 2. If possible, use photos of the children in the classroom. Post near the group-time area for quick reference and use with children.

Plan for Each Time of Your Day

Arrival and Departures

- [ ] Create a daily sign-in sheet for children to write or scribble their names on when they arrive. See *The Creative Curriculum® for Preschool* Intentional Teaching Card LL42, "Daily Sign-In," for ideas.

- [ ] Create a sheet for families to sign their children in and place it next to the children's sheet. Use Intentional Teaching Card SE02, "Look Who's Here," to develop your opening routine.

- [ ] Create an age-appropriate, interactive attendance chart to use at group time.

- [ ] Review Intentional Teaching Card SE07, "Good-Byes," for strategies on supporting children during arrival.

Large Group

- [ ] Decide what will be included in your opening routine. For example, you might sing a welcome song and then review the children's attendance chart before having a group discussion about your study topic. If your program requires you to say the Pledge of Allegiance, you can do this during your opening routine.

- [ ] Review *Mighty Minutes®* for welcome songs, such as "Hello Friends" (M78), that you can use during your opening routine.

- [ ] Determine where to hold your large-group meetings. If your classroom is not large enough to dedicate a separate area for group meetings, use one of the larger interest areas, such as the Block or Library area.

- [ ] Make sure you have access to electrical outlets near the large-group meeting area.

- [ ] Read *The Creative Curriculum® for Preschool, Volume 1: The Foundation,* Chapters 2 and 4 to get a sense of what activities will occur during large-group time. The five teaching guides that complement *Beginning the Year* will explain what to do during each large-group time.

Transitions

- [ ] Talk to other teachers, your coach, or mentor about classroom management during transitions, e.g., cleanup, moving children from place to place, or preparing for rest.

- [ ] Locate the *Mighty Minutes®* cards in *The Creative Curriculum® for Preschool* materials. Begin to learn several of the songs, chants, or simple games to use during transitional times.

Beginning the Year Getting Started

Plan for Each Time of Your Day, continued

Choice Time

- [ ] Read *The Creative Curriculum® for Preschool, Volume 1: The Foundation*, Chapters 2 and 4 about choice time.

- [ ] Decide whether you will use an interest-area management system as suggested in *Volume 1: The Foundation*, Chapter 2, and create the necessary materials.

Read-Aloud

- [ ] Become familiar with the *The Creative Curriculum® for Preschool Book Discussion Cards*™. The teaching guides will tell you when to use the read-aloud strategy with selected books.

- [ ] Refer to *The Creative Curriculum® for Preschool, Volume 3: Literacy* to learn more about various read-aloud techniques.

Small Group

- [ ] Review the guidelines for leading small-group experiences in *The Creative Curriculum® for Preschool, Volume 1: The Foundation*, Chapter 4.

- [ ] Review a few of the *Intentional Teaching Cards*™ to become familiar with their structure.

Meals and Snacks

- [ ] Talk to veteran teachers, your coach, or mentor and refer to *Volume 1: The Foundation*, Chapter 2 about the process and guidelines for mealtimes in your program.

- [ ] Locate where children eat meals and snacks.

- [ ] Locate the child- and adult-size cleanup supplies if meals are served in the classroom. You'll want them readily available.

Caring for Self and the Classroom

- [ ] Make a sign with pictures and words demonstrating the steps for proper hand washing.

- [ ] Learn a hand-washing song or chant to use in the first few weeks as children learn the procedures. Refer to Mighty Minutes M06, "This is the Way."

- [ ] Label cubbies or spaces for each child's belongings. See examples in *Volume 1: The Foundation*, Chapter 2.

☐ Create and post a job chart. Refer to *Volume 1: The Foundation*, Chapter 2 for suggestions on jobs that may be appropriate for your classroom. Review Intentional Teaching Card SE12, "Classroom Jobs."

☐ Find out your program requirements for daily cleanup and sanitation of the classroom.

Rest or Nap Time (full-day programs)

☐ Label cots or mats and supplies for rest time use and determine storage areas.

☐ Locate relaxing music that can be used at the beginning of rest time.

Plan for Ongoing, Observation-Based Assessment

☐ Create a system for recording and storing observation notes. See *The Creative Curriculum® for Preschool, Volume 1: The Foundation*, Chapter 4 for more information and ideas.

☐ Browse through *Volume 6: Objectives for Development & Learning*. Identify the colored band that is associated with the age-group or class/grade you teach. Become familiar with the information related to that colored band.

☐ Review the objectives and dimensions in *Volume 6: Objectives for Development & Learning*.

Now that you've completed the checklist, take some time to review the daily plans included in this *Teaching Guide*. Begin gathering materials needed for choice time and small-group experiences. Browse through the social–emotional section of your *Intentional Teaching Cards*. These cards offer ideas for supporting children as they separate from their families. They also offer guidance strategies that will help you build positive relationships with children and guide their behavior during these first few weeks.

Have a great school year!

Refer to *Guide to The Creative Curriculum® for Preschool* for guidance on weekly planning.

Preparing for Wow! Experiences

The "At a Glance" pages list these suggested Wow! Experiences, which require some advance planning.

Focus Question 1:	Day 5: A Walk Around the School
Focus Question 3:	Day 5: Visit From a Family Member With a Special Skill
Focus Question 5:	Day 2: Visit From a School Worker
	Day 2: Visit From a Family Member to Cook During Choice Time
	Day 3: Visit From a School Worker
Ministudy:	Day 1: Walk Around the School
	Day 3: Interview With a School Worker
	Day 4: Walk Around the School

Focus Questions

AT A GLANCE # Focus Question 1

What names do we need to know at school?

Vocabulary—English: children's names, interest areas, lost, family, skills, portrait, beehive

	Day 1	Day 2	Day 3
Interest Areas	**All:** basic materials	**All:** basic materials	**All:** basic materials
Question of the Day	Can you find your name and put it on the board?	Have you ever lost something?	Did Humpty Dumpty dance, or did he crack?
Large Group	**Rhyme:** "Humpty Dumpty" **Discussion and Shared Writing:** Our Names **Materials:** Intentional Teaching Card SE04, "Actively Listening to Children"; Intentional Teaching Card SE07, "Good-Byes"; Mighty Minutes 81, "Humpty Dumpty"; raw egg in shell; Mighty Minutes 78, "Hello Friends"; name cards with children's pictures	**Rhyme:** Write the poem, "Three Little Kittens," on chart paper. **Discussion and Shared Writing:** Family Names **Materials:** none	**Rhyme:** "Let's Make a Cake" **Discussion and Shared Writing:** Finding Our Names in the Classroom **Materials:** Mighty Minutes 83, "Let's Make a Cake"; alphabet cards; *Anansi and His Children*; Mighty Minutes 40, "Clap a Friend's Name"
Read-Aloud	*A Pocket for Corduroy*	*Love Is a Family*	*Quinito, Day and Night*
Small Group	**Introducing Interest Areas**	**Introducing Interest Areas:** eBook version of *Anansi and His Children*	**Introducing Interest Areas**
Mighty Minutes®	Mighty Minutes 30, "Bounce, Bounce, Bounce"	Mighty Minutes 30, "Bounce, Bounce, Bounce"	Mighty Minutes 40, "Clap a Friend's Name"

Spanish: *se pierdan, familia, destrezas, retrato familiar, colmena*

Day 4	Day 5	Make Time for…
All: basic materials	**Art:** mirrors; collage materials	### Outdoor Experiences **Introducing the Playground** • Take the children on a short tour of the playground. • Each day, talk with the children about a specific area of the playground. Explain basic safety rules, e.g., tricycles must stay on the path.
Do you know how to use this? (Display a magnifying glass or interesting classroom item.)	Do you know the name of this place? (Display a picture of the front of the school.)	
Movement: Bounce, Bounce, Bounce **Discussion and Shared Writing:** Names of Interesting Things in the Classroom **Materials:** Mighty Minutes 30, "Bounce, Bounce, Bounce"; pictures of objects in the classroom	**Poem:** "Move to the Beat" **Discussion and Shared Writing:** Names of Places in the School **Materials:** Mighty Minutes 91, "Move to the Beat"; drum; digital camera	### Family Partnerships • Invite family members to join the class for a walk around the school on day 5. • Ask families to bring in family photos to display in the classroom. • Invite families to access the eBook, *Anansi and His Children*. ### Wow! Experiences • Day 5: A walk around the school to learn the names of different places
Love Is a Family	*Wemberly Worried* Book Discussion Card 20 (first read-aloud)	**Outdoor supervision is especially important during the first few weeks of school, as children learn their way around the area and explore unfamiliar play structures.**
Introducing Interest Areas	**Introducing Interest Areas**	
Mighty Minutes 75, "Busy Bees"; basket of common classroom items	Mighty Minutes 81, "Humpty Dumpty"; egg shakers or maracas	

Day 1 Focus Question 1

What names do we need to know at school?

Vocabulary
the children's names and interest areas

Question of the Day: Can you find your name and put it on the board?

Large Group

Greet each child and his or her family upon arrival. See Intentional Teaching Cards SE04, "Actively Listening to Children" and SE07, "Good-Byes," for strategies to help you support children who have a difficult time separating from their families.

Opening Routine

- Sing a welcome song and talk about who's here.

See Intentional Teaching Card SE02, "Look Who's Here!" for attendance chart ideas.

Rhyme: "Humpty Dumpty"

- Use Mighty Minutes 81, "Humpty Dumpty." Follow the guidance on the card.

Discussion and Shared Writing: Our Names

- Say, "*Humpty Dumpty* is such an interesting name for an egg. Everybody in our class has an interesting name, too. Let's learn each other's names!"

- Talk about the question of the day located on the "At a Glance" chart.
- Review Mighty Minutes 78, "Hello Friends," and follow the guidance on the card.
- As you sing, show each child his or her name card (with picture) or write each child's name on a chart.
- Explain, "Each part of our classroom has a name, too. Today, we will walk around our classroom and find out the names of the different areas."

Before transitioning to interest areas, walk around the room with the children and briefly describe each area, e.g., say, "This is the Dramatic Play area. We have dress-up clothes, dishes, and baby dolls here for pretending." Keep children's name cards (picture and name) in a basket. To transition to the interest areas, pull out names one at a time and have each child choose an area to explore. If that area is already full, ask the child to select another area.

See *The Creative Curriculum for Preschool, Volume 2: Interest Areas* for ideas on how to set up interest areas for the beginning of the year.

Beginning the Year Focus Questions

Choice Time

As you interact with children in the interest areas, make time to

- Help children choose an area of the room to explore and show them how to use materials appropriately.

> At the beginning of the year, the materials in the interest areas should be very familiar to children. Gradually introduce new materials. Show children how to use them and where to store them.

Read-Aloud

Read *A Pocket for Corduroy*.

- **Before you read**, show the cover and read the title. Ask, "Has anyone heard this story before?"
- **As you read**, talk about how Corduroy feels in the story.
- **After you read**, ask, "Why did Lisa put his name in his pocket?"

> **English-language learners**
> When possible, use children's home languages to introduce the book that you plan to read aloud. Seek help from colleagues, volunteers, or parents if you do not speak the children's languages.

Small Group

Introducing Interest Areas

- Select an interest area to introduce to the children.
- Describe the materials in the area and invite children to explore them.
- Talk about how children may play with the materials.
- Explain to and show children how to clean up the area when they are finished, e.g., say, "Each basket has a picture and words on it. This is a picture of star builders, and these words say *star builders*. That's how I know to put the star builders in this basket. The shelf is labeled with the same picture and words. That's how I know to put the basket on the shelf."

> You may want to start with the Dramatic Play area because the materials there are most like what children might find in their homes. Children feel more secure in familiar settings, which increases their confidence to try new things and express themselves.

Mighty Minutes®

- Use Mighty Minutes 30, "Bounce, Bounce, Bounce." Follow the guidance on the card.

Large-Group Roundup

- Recall the day's events.
- Invite children to share something they enjoyed exploring during choice time.

Day 2 — Focus Question 1

What names do we need to know at school?

Vocabulary
English: *lost, family*
Spanish: *se pierdan, familia*
Question of the Day: Have you ever lost something?

Large Group

Opening Routine

- Sing a welcome song and talk about who's here.

Rhyme: "Three Little Kittens"

- Recite the "Three Little Kittens." For the words, see the next page.

Discussion and Shared Writing: Finding Our Names in the Classroom

- Say, "I wonder how the three little kittens *lost* their mittens."
- Discuss children's responses.
- Talk about the question of the day.
- Explain, "In our classroom we have somewhere special to put our things so they don't get *lost*." Talk about children's individual storage spaces, such as cubbies. Point out that each space is labeled with a child's name. Invite children to find their cubbies and explore what's inside them.
- Say, "We can find our names in other places in the classroom, too. Let's walk around and investigate the places where we can find our names."
- After walking around, gather children in the large-group area. Ask, "Where did you find your names in our classroom?"
- Record children's responses.
- Tell children why their names are posted in each place, e.g., say, "Your names are in the Library area so you can look at them to help you remember how to write your name."

English-language learners
Establishing routines, such as always putting things in cubbies, helps all children know what is expected of them. It also helps them participate in daily activities and understand the language used to talk about classroom events.

Before transitioning to interest areas, explain, "After you do artwork in the classroom, you may want to take it home and share it with your *family*. Put your artwork in your cubby so you'll remember to take it home with you." Invite children to draw pictures in the Art area and then store their work in their cubbies to take home later.

Beginning the Year Focus Questions

Choice Time	As you interact with children in the interest areas, make time to • Talk with children as they draw pictures in the Art area. • Ask, "What can you tell me about your picture?"	• Observe how children use the materials and represent their ideas in their pictures. • As needed, continue to help children make choices and use materials in all the interest areas.
Read-Aloud	Read *Love Is a Family*. • **Before you read**, show the cover of the book and ask, "What do you think this story is about?" • **As you read**, take time to respond to children's comments and questions as they relate the story to their own families.	• **After you read**, look back through the pages and talk about the families in the story. Point out the differences in the families' sizes. Ask, "Do you have a big *family* or a small *family*?"
Small Group	**Introducing Interest Areas** • Select an interest area to introduce to the children. • Describe the materials in the area and invite children to explore them.	• Talk about how children may use the materials in their play. • Show children how to clean up the area when they are finished.
Mighty Minutes®	• Use Mighty Minutes 30, "Bounce, Bounce, Bounce." Follow the guidance on the card.	• Recall the day's events. • Invite children who drew pictures in the Art area to talk about their work.
Large-Group Roundup		

> **Three Little Kittens**
>
> *Three little kittens lost their mittens,*
> *And they began to cry.*
> *"Oh, mother dear, see here, see here,*
> *Our mittens we have lost."*
> *"What? Lost your mittens, you sad little kittens!*
> *Let's search for them close by.*
> *Meow, meow, meow."*
>
> *The three little kittens soon found their mittens,*
> *And they began to sigh.*
> *"Oh, mother dear, see here, see here,*
> *Our mittens we have found."*
> *"Put on your mittens, you silly little kittens.*
> *Now let's go have some pie.*
> *Purr, purr, purr.*
> *Hmmm, I smell a rat close by."*

Day 3 Focus Question 1

What names do we need to know at school?

Bobby   Aneesa   Kumar   Alejandro

Vocabulary
English: *skills, portrait*
Spanish: *destrezas, retrato familiar*
Question of the Day: Did Humpty Dumpty dance, or did he crack?

Large Group

Opening Routine

- Sing a welcome song and talk about who's here.

Rhyme: "Let's Make a Cake"

- Use Mighty Minutes 83, "Let's Make a Cake."
- Try the variation on the back of the card to encourage children to write the letters with their fingers.

Discussion and Shared Writing: Finding Our Names in the Classroom

- Read *Anansi and His Children*.
- Say, "Anansi's children have interesting names, just like Humpty Dumpty's. All of Anansi's children have names that describe their *skills*, or things they can do well."
- Record the names of Anansi's children as you say them.

English-language learners
When possible, use nonverbal communication techniques, such as pointing to names and pictures. These cues are particularly helpful for English-language learners to understand the meaning of words.

Before transitioning to interest areas, show a page from *Anansi and His Children* that shows a picture of the whole family. Say, "This is a picture of Anansi's family. It's a family *portrait*." Talk about the materials in the Art area. Explain that children may use them to make family *portraits*.

Consider using Mighty Minutes 40, "Clap a Friend's Name," or another name game, to transition children from large-group time to interest areas. Using children's names frequently in songs and games during the first few weeks of school helps children learn each other's names.

Beginning the Year Focus Questions

Choice Time

As you interact with children in the interest areas, make time to

- Talk with children as they work on their family portraits.
- Ask, "What can you tell me about your picture? What are the names of the people in your picture?"

> This activity offers children an opportunity to talk about their families. While children may not yet be able to draw recognizable representations, what they say about their artwork is so important during this first week. When children say, "Here's my cat," "My mom's away on a Navy ship," or "My grandma lives with us," you learn invaluable information about the children in your room.
>
> For more information about how children's skills for painting and drawing develop, see *The Creative Curriculum® for Preschool, Volume 2: Interest Areas.*

Read-Aloud

Read *Quinito, Day and Night*.

- **Before you read**, explain, "Quinito is the name of the boy in this story. This book is about all of the things he does during his day."

- **As you read**, invite children to relate the events in Quinito's day to the events in their own day.
- **After you read**, say, "Quinito's family sings him a song before he goes to sleep at night." Ask, "What do you do before you go to sleep at night?"

Small Group

Introducing Interest Areas

- Select an interest area to introduce to the children. You may want to choose the Technology area so you can show the children how to access and read the book *Anansi and His Children*.

- Describe the materials in the area and invite children to explore them.
- Talk about how children may use the materials in their play.
- Show children how to clean up the area when they are finished.

Mighty Minutes®

- Use Mighty Minutes 40, "Clap a Friend's Name." Follow the guidance on the card.

Large-Group Roundup

- Recall the day's events.
- Invite children who made family portraits during choice time to share their work.

The Creative Curriculum® for Preschool

Day 4 — Focus Question 1

What names do we need to know at school?

Bobby   Aneesa   Kumar   Alejandro

Vocabulary

English: *beehive*

Spanish: *colmena*

Question of the Day: Do you know how to use this? (Display a magnifying glass or interesting classroom item.)

Large Group

Opening Routine

- Sing a welcome song and talk about who's here.

Movement: Bounce, Bounce, Bounce

- Use Mighty Minutes 30, "Bounce, Bounce, Bounce." Follow the guidance on the card.

Discussion and Shared Writing: Names of Interesting Things in the Classroom

- Talk about the question of the day.
- Explain, "There are so many things to discover in our classroom."
- Show a picture of an interesting classroom item, such as a water fountain or sculpting tool for clay.
- Ask, "What do you think this is?"
- Record children's ideas.
- Invite a child to match the picture with the actual item in the classroom.
- Continue the game using other pictures until all of the items have been named and located or until the children lose interest in the game.

Before transitioning to interest areas, talk about the materials in the Art area and how children may use them to finish their family portraits.

Choice Time

As you interact with children in the interest areas, make time to

- Talk with children as they work on their family portraits.
- Ask, "What can you tell me about your picture?"
- Talk with children about their families.
- Observe how children use the materials. Note their ability to represent their ideas in pictures.

Beginning the Year Focus Questions

Read-Aloud

Read *Love Is a Family.*

- **Before you read**, ask, "Who remembers what this book is about?"
- **As you read**, count the individuals in each family described in the story.
- **After you read**, ask, "How many persons are in your family?" Help children count their family members, e.g., say, "Michael said he lives with his mommy and grandpa. That's Michael [hold up one finger], his mommy [hold up a second finger], and his grandpa [hold up a third finger]. So there are one, two, three persons in Michael's family."

Small Group

Introducing Interest Areas

- Select an interest area to introduce to the children.
- Describe the materials in the area and invite children to explore them.
- Talk about how children may use the materials in their play.
- Show children how to clean up the area when they are finished.

English-language learners
Label shelves and containers in children's home languages. Having environmental print in the home languages of English-language learners helps them participate and feel proud of their culture and families. Use a different color for each language, and use that color consistently throughout the classroom.

Mighty Minutes®

- Use Mighty Minutes 75, "Busy Bees." Try the color variation on the back of the card.
- Say, "We're going to pretend the classroom is a *beehive*. A *beehive* is a place where a family of bees lives."
- Pass around a basket of common classroom materials a few times or until children lose interest.
- Invite children to buzz around and put things away to practice returning items to their correct locations.

Large-Group Roundup

- Recall the day's events.
- Invite children who worked on family portraits during choice time to share their work.
- Tell children they will be taking a walk around the school tomorrow.

Day 5 — Focus Question 1

What names do we need to know at school?

Vocabulary

English: See *Book Discussion Card 20, Wemberly Worried* (*Prudencia se preocupa*), for words.

Question of the Day: Do you know the name of this place? (Display a picture of the front of the school.)

Large Group

Opening Routine

- Sing a welcome song and talk about who's here.

Poem: "Move to the Beat"

- Use Mighty Minutes 91, "Move to the Beat." Follow the guidance on the card.

Discussion and Shared Writing: Names of Places in the School

- Explain, "We know each other's names. We know the names of the areas in our classroom. And we know the names of many of the materials in our classroom."
- Talk about the question of the day.
- Say, "Today we're going to walk around our school to learn the names of the special places here."
- Ask, "What do you think we will see on our walk today?"
- Record children's responses.

> Take pictures of the places you visit. Use the photos to create a display or book to remind children of the names of the places.

Before transitioning to interest areas, talk about the mirrors and collage materials in the Art area and how children may use them to create self-portraits.

Choice Time

As you interact with children in the interest areas, make time to

- Talk with them about their self-portraits.
- Invite them to look in the mirrors. Then talk with them about their characteristics.
- Invite children to write their names on separate labels. Create a display of children's self-portraits and written names.

> Be sure to save the self-portraits and writing samples in each child's portfolio. Collect similar samples throughout the year so families can see their children's progress over time.

Beginning the Year Focus Questions

Read-Aloud

Read *Wemberly Worried*.

- Use Book Discussion Card 20, *Wemberly Worried*. Follow the guidance for the first read-aloud.
- **After you read**, see "Supporting Social–Emotional Development" on the back of the *Book Discussion Card* for additional questions to ask.

> The *Book Discussion Cards* are designed for repeated use. Since this is the beginning of the year, keep the discussions simple and limit your questions and comments. As the year progresses, you may want to return to the book and ask increasingly complex questions.

Small Group

Introducing Interest Areas

- Select an interest area to introduce to the children.
- Describe the materials in the area and invite children to explore them.
- Talk about how children may use the materials in their play.
- Show children how to clean up the area when they are finished.

> Repeating this experience for several days helps familiarize children with each interest area.

Mighty Minutes®

- Use Mighty Minutes 81, "Humpty Dumpty." Try the instrumental or beat version on the back of the card.

Large-Group Roundup

- Recall the day's events.
- Invite children who worked on self-portraits to share their work. Invite them to describe the materials they used.

AT A GLANCE

Focus Question 2

What should we do if we get sad or scared at school?

Vocabulary—English: *tempo, real, pretend, scared*

	Day 1	Day 2
Interest Areas	**Toys and Games:** puzzles	**Library:** a personal journal for each child (newsprint pages with construction paper covers); variety of writing tools
Question of the Day	Have you ever been sad?	Have you ever been scared?
Large Group	**Movement:** Dance With Scarves **Discussion and Shared Writing:** Feeling Sad **Materials:** music or drum; scarf or piece of fabric; *The Kissing Hand;* Intentional Teaching Card SE03, "Calm-Down Place"	**Rhyme:** "Little Miss Muffet" **Discussion and Shared Writing:** Feeling Scared **Materials:** Mighty Minutes 90, "Little Miss Muffet"; fake or paper spider; Intentional Teaching Card LL39, "My Daily Journal"
Read-Aloud	*Wemberly Worried* Book Discussion Card 20 (second read-aloud)	*The Kissing Hand*
Small Group	Introducing Interest Areas	Introducing Interest Areas
Mighty Minutes®	Mighty Minutes 87, "One, Two, Buckle My Shoe"	Mighty Minutes 46, "Strolling Through the Park"

Spanish: *ritmo, de verdad, de juguete, asustado*

Day 3	Make Time for…
Art: safety scissors (right- and left-handed); paper; thick marker	### Outdoor Experiences **Introducing Outdoor Materials** - Introduce toys and other materials that are frequently used outside, e.g., balls, hula hoops, and dump trucks in the sandbox.
What makes you happy?	### Family Partnerships
Rhyme: "Two Plump Armadillos" **Discussion and Shared Writing:** Feelings at School **Materials:** Mighty Minutes 44, "Two Plump Armadillos"; Intentional Teaching Card SE06, "Talk About Feelings"; Intentional Teaching Card P08, "Cutting with Scissors"	- Ask families to continue bringing in family photos. - Talk to families whose children find it particularly challenging to transition from home to school in the morning. See Intentional Teaching Card SE07, "Good-Byes," for ideas on helping families create good-bye rituals.
Wemberly Worried Book Discussion Card 20 (third read-aloud)	**English-language learners** **Plan activities with family members of English-language learners. Encourage them to use their home languages in the classroom during the activities. The presence of family members can help build children's confidence in social situations and their comfort in the classroom.**
Introducing Interest Areas	
Mighty Minutes 46, "Strolling Through the Park"	

Day 1 — Focus Question 2

What should we do if we get sad or scared at school?

Vocabulary

English: *tempo*; See *Book Discussion Card 20, Wemberly Worried (Prudencia se preocupa),* for additional words.
Spanish: *ritmo*
Question of the Day: Have you ever been sad?

Large Group

Opening Routine

- Sing a welcome song and talk about who's here.

Movement: Dance With Scarves

- Explain, "We're going to move our bodies to the *tempo*, or speed, of the music."
- Play slow music or beat a drum slowly. Ask, "How should we move to this music?"
- Play fast music or beat a drum quickly. Ask, "How should we move to this music?"
- Give each child a scarf or piece of fabric.
- Explain, "Let's move our bodies and our scarves to the *tempo* of the music."
- Play music and invite children to move to the *tempo*.

English-language learners
While open-ended questions encourage children's thinking, asking too many of them may be too difficult for English-language learners to answer, especially at the beginning of the year. Ask closed questions that children can answer by pointing to pictures or saying one word, e.g., "Should we move slowly or quickly?" For this activity, you may also want to demonstrate the movements while saying *quickly* or *slowly*, as appropriate.

Discussion and Shared Writing: Feeling Sad

- Read *The Kissing Hand*.
- After you read, ask, "Why was Chester sad? What did his mother do to make him feel better?"
- Talk about the question of the day. Ask, "What makes you feel sad?"
- Record children's responses.
- Explain, "Everyone is sad sometimes." Ask, "What are some things you can do if you ever feel sad at school?" Reassure children that you and other adults in the classroom are there to support them.

Review Intentional Teaching Card SE03, "Calm-Down Place." Show children the quiet place to go in your classroom when they need time away from the group.

Before transitioning to interest areas, show some of the puzzles in the Toys and Games area. Invite children to work on them during choice time.

Beginning the Year Focus Questions

Choice Time

As you interact with children in the interest areas, make time to

- Observe them as they work with puzzles in the Toys and Games area.
- Describe the strategies they are using to complete the puzzles, e.g., "I notice that you turned that piece three times to find the matching side."

> **For strategies to support children's puzzle skills, see Intentional Teaching Card M23, "Putting Puzzles Together."**

Read-Aloud

Read *Wemberly Worried*.

- Use Book Discussion Card 20, *Wemberly Worried*. Follow the guidance for the second read-aloud.

Small Group

Introducing Interest Areas

- Select an interest area to introduce to the children.
- Describe the materials in the area and invite children to explore them.
- Talk about the ways children may use the materials in their play.
- Show children how to clean up the area when they are finished.

Mighty Minutes®

- Use Mighty Minutes 87, "One, Two, Buckle My Shoe." Follow the guidance on the card.

Large-Group Roundup

- Recall the day's events.
- Invite children who worked on puzzles to show one that they put together.

Day 2 — Focus Question 2

What should we do if we get sad or scared at school?

Vocabulary
English: *real, pretend, scared*
Spanish: *de verdad, de juguete, asustado*
Question of the Day: Have you ever been scared?

Large Group

Opening Routine

- Sing a welcome song and talk about who's here.

Rhyme: "Little Miss Muffet"

- Use Mighty Minutes 90, "Little Miss Muffet." Follow the guidance on the card.

Discussion and Shared Writing: Feeling Scared

- Show children a fake spider or one cut out of paper. Ask, "Is this real or pretend? How do you know?"
- Explain, "Like Little Miss Muffet, some people are afraid of real spiders."
- Review the question of the day. Ask, "What makes you feel scared?"
- Record children's responses.
- Say, "Show me what your face looks like when you're scared."
- Ask, "What can you do if you feel scared at school?" Reassure children that you, as well as the other adults in the room, will help them if they ever feel scared.

Before transitioning to interest areas, explain, "Yesterday, we talked about feeling sad. Today, we talked about feeling scared. Sometimes when people feel sad or scared, they feel better when they draw or write about their feelings." Show them their journals or where they can find paper and pencils in the Library or Art areas. During choice time, invite children to write or draw pictures of something that makes them sad or scared.

> See Intentional Teaching Card LL39, "My Daily Journal," for more information about using journals in your classroom.

Beginning the Year Focus Questions

Choice Time

As you interact with children in the interest areas, make time to

- Talk with them about their feelings.
- Invite them to draw or write about their feelings.
- Record children's dictation about their drawings, as appropriate.

English-language learners
English-language learners and English-speaking children can benefit from interacting with each other during choice-time activities. Hearing their classmates use English as they talk about their feelings or draw pictures helps English-language learners develop oral language competency.

Read-Aloud

Read *The Kissing Hand*.

- **Before you read**, ask, "Who can remember what this book is about?"
- **As you read**, point out how school seemed strange and scary to Chester before he started.
- **After you read**, say, "Chester was really worried when he started school." Ask, "What made Chester feel better about leaving his mother?"

English-language learners
Rereading a book several times helps all children gain additional understanding
of unfamiliar words and phrases.

Small Group

Introducing Interest Areas

- Select an interest area to introduce to the children.
- Describe the materials available in the area and invite children to explore them.
- Talk about how children may use the materials in their play.
- Show children how to clean up the area when they are finished.

Mighty Minutes®

- Use Mighty Minutes 46, "Strolling Through the Park." Follow the guidance on the card.

Large-Group Roundup

- Recall the day's events.
- Invite children to talk about something they enjoyed doing during choice time.

Day 3 — Focus Question 2

What should we do if we get sad or scared at school?

Vocabulary

English: See *Book Discussion Card* 20, *Wemberly Worried* (*Prudencia se preocupa*), for words.

Question of the Day: What makes you happy?

Large Group

Opening Routine

- Sing a welcome song and talk about who's here.

Rhyme: "Two Plump Armadillos"

- Use Mighty Minutes 44, "Two Plump Armadillos." Follow the guidance on the card.

Discussion and Shared Writing: Feelings at School

- Talk about the question of the day.
- Review Intentional Teaching Card SE06, "Talk About Feelings." Follow the guidance on the card.
- As you talk about each feeling, ask, "When might you feel this way at school?"
- Record children's responses.

Before transitioning to interest areas, talk about the scissors and paper in the Art area and how children may use them to practice cutting.

> See Intentional Teaching Card P08, "Cutting With Scissors," for more information about children working with scissors.

Choice Time

As you interact with children in the interest areas, make time to

- Observe children's ability to cut with scissors.

Beginning the Year Focus Questions

Read-Aloud

Read *Wemberly Worried.*

- Use Book Discussion Card 20, *Wemberly Worried.* Follow the guidance for the third read-aloud.

Small Group

Introducing Interest Areas

- Select an interest area to introduce to the children.
- Describe the materials in the area and invite children to explore them.
- Talk about how children may use the materials in their play.
- Show children how to clean up the area when they are finished.

English-language learners
Ask parents or family members for a few key words or phrases in the children's home languages, such as words for *eat, listen,* and *table.* Use these words to communicate with children, especially early in the school year when many are using only their home languages in class.

Mighty Minutes®

- Use Mighty Minutes 46, "Strolling Through the Park." Follow the guidance on the card.

Large-Group Roundup

- Recall the day's events.
- Invite children to share something they enjoyed doing during choice time today.

The Creative Curriculum® for Preschool

AT A GLANCE **Focus Question 3**

What are our rules?

Vocabulary—English: *rule, resting position, question, recommendation*

	Day 1	Day 2	Day 3
Interest Areas	**Blocks:** cars and trucks	**Dramatic Play:** dress-up clothes **Technology:** eBook version of *A World of Families*	**Music and Movement:** instruments; basket
Question of the Day	Did you wash your hands when you got to school?	Would you like to paint today?	What song shall we sing today? (Offer two choices.)
Large Group	**Song:** "Mary Had a Little Lamb" **Discussion and Shared Writing:** Why We Have Rules **Materials:** Mighty Minutes 13, "Simon Says"; digital camera	**Game:** Jack in the Box **Discussion and Shared Writing:** Writing the Rules **Materials:** Mighty Minutes 74, "Jack in the Box"; Intentional Teaching Card SE09, "Big Rule, Little Rule"	**Chant:** "Are You Ready?" **Discussion and Shared Writing:** Playing Instruments **Materials:** Mighty Minutes 73, "Are You Ready?"; basket of musical instruments
Read-Aloud	*Charlie Anderson* Book Discussion Card 17 (first read-aloud)	*A World of Families*	*Charlie Anderson* Book Discussion Card 17 (second read-aloud)
Small Group	Introducing Interest Areas	**Option 1: Modeling Clay** Intentional Teaching Card M52, "Modeling Clay" (See card for equipment, ingredients, and recipe.) **Option 2: Black Bean Corn Salad** Intentional Teaching Card M53, "Black Bean Corn Salad" (See card for equipment, ingredients, and recipe.)	**Option 1: The Name Game** Intentional Teaching Card LL47, "The Name Game"; children's names on sentence strips; basket or other container; blank strip of paper or index card **Option 2: Making My Name** Intentional Teaching Card LL29, "Making My Name"; small, sturdy envelopes; letter manipulatives; marker
Mighty Minutes®	Mighty Minutes 94, "Old MacDonald"	Mighty Minutes 94, "Old MacDonald"; real instruments (optional)	Mighty Minutes 44, "Two Plump Armadillos"

Spanish: *regla, posición de descanso, pregunta, recomendación*

Day 4	Day 5	Make Time for...
Music and Movement: instruments	**Library:** books about families	**Outdoor Experiences** **Physical Fun** • Use Intentional Teaching Card P12, "Exploring Pathways." Follow the guidance on the card.
How many fingers are on your hand? Two or five?	Have you ever seen someone _____? (Name the special skill of today's visitor.)	**Family Partnerships** • Invite a family member to visit the classroom on day 5 to demonstrate something special that she can do with her hands, e.g., play an instrument, make pottery, juggle, knit, or carve. • Invite families to access the eBook, *A World of Families*.
Movement: Move to the Beat **Discussion and Shared Writing:** What Can We Do With Our Hands? **Materials:** Mighty Minutes 91, "Move to the Beat"; drum; Mighty Minutes 26, "Echo Clapping" **Materials for Large-Group Roundup:** Intentional Teaching Card LL54, "Asking Questions"	**Chant:** "Are You Ready?" **Discussion and Shared Writing:** Family Member Visit **Materials:** Mighty Minutes 73, "Are You Ready?"; several books about families	**Wow! Experiences** • Day 5: Visit from a family member with a special skill
Peeny Butter Fudge	*Charlie Anderson* Book Discussion Card 17 (third read-aloud)	**English-language learners** Each family is unique, so you will need to use a variety of ways to communicate with the families in your program. Over time, learn as much as you can from and about them. Help each other understand cultural differences and encourage family members to share their interests and expertise.
Option 1: Can You Find It? Intentional Teaching Card M51, "Can You Find It?"; common classroom objects **Option 2: Where Does It Belong?** Intentional Teaching Card M51, "Can You Find It?"; common classroom objects; digital camera	**Option 1: Can You Find It?** Intentional Teaching Card M51, "Can You Find It?"; common classroom objects **Option 2: Where Does It Belong?** Intentional Teaching Card M51, "Can You Find It?"; common classroom objects; digital camera	
Mighty Minutes 87, "One, Two, Buckle My Shoe"	Mighty Minutes 87, "One, Two, Buckle My Shoe"	

Day 1   Focus Question 3

What are our rules?

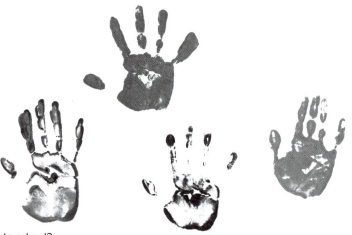

Vocabulary
English: rule; See *Book Discussion Card 17, Charlie Anderson* (*Charlie Anderson*), for additional words.
Spanish: regla
Question of the Day: Did you wash your hands when you got to school?

Large Group

Opening Routine
- Sing a welcome song and talk about who's here.

Song: "Mary Had a Little Lamb"
- Sing "Mary Had a Little Lamb" with the children.

Discussion and Shared Writing: Why We Have Rules
- Repeat the following line in "Mary Had a Little Lamb": "He followed her to school one day, which was against the rules."
- Ask, "What are *rules*?"
- Record children's responses.
- Ask, "Why do we have *rules*?"
- Record children's responses.
- Ask, "Why do you think it's a *rule* at Mary's school that pets aren't allowed to come to school with the children?"
- Talk about the question of the day. Ask, "Why do you think it's a rule to wash our hands when we get to school?"
- Explain, "We're going to play a game. This game has *rules* we have to follow, just like Mary had *rules* to follow."
- Lead the children in a game of "Simon Says." Review Mighty Minutes 13, "Simon Says," and follow the guidance on the card.

Before transitioning to interest areas, talk about the cars and trucks in the Block area and how children may use them.

Choice Time

As you interact with children in the interest areas, make time to

- Observe children as they play in the Block area.
- Talk to the children about their structures by describing what you see, e.g., "I see you used all of the long, rectangular blocks and lined them up."
- Take photos of children's structures.

> **Including props and accessories in the Block area encourages children to expand their block play into dramatic play.**

Beginning the Year Focus Questions

Read-Aloud

Read *Charlie Anderson*.

- Use Book Discussion Card 17, *Charlie Anderson*. Follow the guidance for the first read-aloud.

- **After you read**, see "Supporting Social–Emotional Development" on the back of the card for additional questions to ask.

Small Group

Introducing Interest Areas

- Select an interest area to introduce to the children.

- Describe the materials in the area and invite children to explore them.

- Talk about how children may use the materials in their play.

- Show children how to clean up the area when they are finished.

Mighty Minutes®

- Use Mighty Minutes 94, "Old MacDonald." Follow the guidance on the card.

Large-Group Roundup

- Recall the day's events.

- Invite children who worked in the Block area to describe the structures they built. If you are able to print the photos you took during choice time, share them with the group as well.

The Creative Curriculum® for Preschool

Day 2 Focus Question 3

What are our rules?

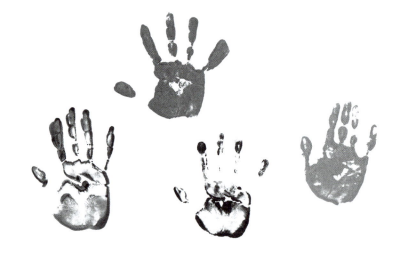

Vocabulary
English: *rule*
Spanish: *regla*
Question of the Day: Would you like to paint today?

Large Group

Opening Routine
- Sing a welcome song and talk about who's here.

Game: Jack in the Box
- Use Mighty Minutes 74, "Jack in the Box." Follow the guidance on the card.

Discussion and Shared Writing: Writing the Rules
- Explain, "Our classroom needs to be a place where everyone feels safe. Yesterday we talked about what a *rule* is. Let's think of some *rules* we should have in our classroom."
- See Intentional Teaching Card SE09, "Big Rule, Little Rule."
- Follow the guidance on the card for generating and enforcing classroom rules.

Before transitioning to interest areas, talk about the dress-up clothes in the Dramatic Play area and how children may use them. Review the question of the day. Show the children who would like to paint today how to create a sign-up sheet with their names so they may have a turn at the easel.

Choice Time

As you interact with children in the interest areas, make time to

- Observe children as they play in the Dramatic Play area.
- Comment on or ask questions about what you see, e.g., "You're wearing work boots and a jacket. Where are you going?"

> By talking about how children play, you make them more aware that they are pretending.

Beginning the Year Focus Questions

Read-Aloud

Read *A World of Families*.

- **Before you read**, show the cover and ask, "What are these families doing?"
- **As you read**, invite children to talk about how the book relates to their own families.
- **After you read**, ask, "What do you like to do with your family?" Record their ideas. Tell the children that the book will be available to them on the computer in the Technology area.

Small Group

Option 1: Modeling Clay

- Use Intentional Teaching Card M52, "Modeling Clay." Follow the guidance on the card.

Option 2: Black Bean Corn Salad

- Use Intentional Teaching Card M53, "Black Bean Corn Salad." Follow the guidance on the card.

English-language learners
When creating small groups, include English-language learners along with English-speaking children. Help children interact with each other. Guide conversations during the activities so that children have visual cues about the meaning of words.

Mighty Minutes®

- Use Mighty Minutes 94, "Old MacDonald." Try the band version on the back of the card using real or imaginary instruments.

Large-Group Roundup

- Recall the day's events.
- Invite children who played with dress-up clothes in the Dramatic Play area to talk about what they did.

The Creative Curriculum® for Preschool

Day 3 Focus Question 3

What are our rules?

Vocabulary
English: *resting position;* See *Book Discussion Card* 17, *Charlie Anderson* (Charlie Anderson), for additional words.
Spanish: *posición de descanso*
Question of the Day: What song shall we sing today? (Offer two choices.)

Large Group

Opening Routine

- Sing a welcome song and talk about who's here.

Chant: "Are You Ready?"

- Use Mighty Minutes 73, "Are You Ready?" Follow the guidance on the card.

Discussion and Shared Writing: Playing Instruments

- Pass around a basket of musical instruments.
- Invite children to select an instrument from the basket. If this is too difficult for some children, hold two instruments in front of each child and ask, "Which one of these instruments would you like to use today?"
- Remind children that later, during choice time, they may play another instrument.
- Explain, "An important rule for playing musical instruments is to learn the *resting position*."
- Show children how to hold their instruments in a resting position, placing the instrument in their laps without playing it, until everyone is ready to play them.
- On an instrument, play the beat to a familiar tune, such as "Mary Had a Little Lamb." Invite the children to play along.

> When you teach children to hold the instrument in a resting position, you are helping them control their impulse to beat a drum or shake a tambourine. Controlling impulses is part of building self-regulation.

Before transitioning to interest areas, tell children that the instruments will be available in the Music and Movement area for them to use during choice time.

Choice Time

As you interact with children in the interest areas, make time to

- Observe children as they play instruments in the Music and Movement area.
- Talk with them about the sounds the different instruments make.

Beginning the Year Focus Questions

Read-Aloud

Read *Charlie Anderson*.

- Use Book Discussion Card 17, *Charlie Anderson*. Follow the guidance for the second read-aloud.

Small Group

Option 1: The Name Game

- Use Intentional Teaching Card LL47, "The Name Game." Follow the guidance on the card.

Option 2: Making My Name

- Use Intentional Teaching Card LL29, "Making My Name." Follow the guidance on the card.

> For more information on supporting children's alphabet knowledge, see *The Creative Curriculum for Preschool*, Volume 3: *Literacy*, Chapter 1.

Mighty Minutes®

- Use Mighty Minutes 44, "Two Plump Armadillos." Follow the guidance on the card.

Large-Group Roundup

- Recall the day's events.
- Talk about the question of the day and sing the song that the children selected earlier.

Day 4 — Focus Question 3

What are our rules?

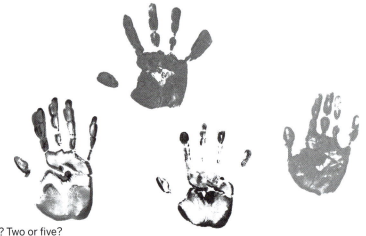

Vocabulary
English: *question*
Spanish: *pregunta*
Question of the Day: How many fingers are on your hand? Two or five?

Large Group

Opening Routine

- Sing a welcome song and talk about who's here.

Movement: Move to the Beat

- Use Mighty Minutes 91, "Move to the Beat." Try the singing version on the back of the card.

English-language learners
As you review the question of the day and hold up the correct number of fingers, say the numbers *two* and *five* in the children's home languages as well as in English. Then have the children repeat each number in the various home languages while holding up the correct number of fingers. This activity helps English-language learners feel included and introduces new languages to other children.

Discussion and Shared Writing: What Can We Do With Our Hands?

- Talk about the question of the day.
- Review Mighty Minutes 26, "Echo Clapping." Follow the guidance on the card.
- Explain, "We can clap with our hands."
- Ask, "What else can we do with our hands at school?"
- Record children's responses on a chart.
- If children offer suggestions that contradict the rules, add to the chart a column called, "Things we don't do with our hands at school." If appropriate, talk about why these things might be harmful or dangerous.

Before transitioning to interest areas, remind children about the instruments in the Music and Movement area and how children may use them with their hands.

Choice Time

As you interact with children in the interest areas, make time to

- Get to know each child better and build relationships. Talk about a child's home life and favorite activities.

Beginning the Year Focus Questions

Read-Aloud

Read *Peeny Butter Fudge*.

- **Before you read**, show the cover of the book and read the title. Ask, "What do you think this book is about?"

- **As you read**, help the children understand the illustration on the page where the mother remembers making the fudge with her own mother.

- **After you read**, check children's predictions.

Small Group

Option 1: Can You Find It?

- Use Intentional Teaching Card M51, "Can You Find It?"
- Follow the guidance on the card using a collection of common classroom objects.

Option 2: Where Does It Belong?

- Use Intentional Teaching Card M51, "Can You Find It?"
- Follow the guidance on the card using a collection of common classroom objects.
- Take photos of the places where children find the objects and where they put them away.
- Make a book using the photos. e.g., "Scissors don't belong in the Block area. Scissors do belong in the Art area."

Mighty Minutes®

- Use Mighty Minutes 87, "One, Two, Buckle My Shoe." Try the instrumental version on the back of the card.

Large-Group Roundup

- Recall the day's events.
- Explain, "Someone will be coming to our classroom tomorrow." Talk about the skill that the person will demonstrate with her hands, e.g., cooking, playing an instrument, or building something.
- Invite children to generate questions to ask the visitor, e.g., "What question would you like to ask our visitor about playing the guitar?"
- Help children verbalize their questions. For example, when a child says, "Guitars are too big to hold," you might respond, "You think guitars are too big to hold. Let's ask her the *question*, 'How do you hold a big guitar?'"

> **Generating questions is an important skill that children will need to investigate study topics throughout the year. See Intentional Teaching Card LL54, "Asking Questions," for more guidance.**

Day 5 Focus Question 3

What are our rules?

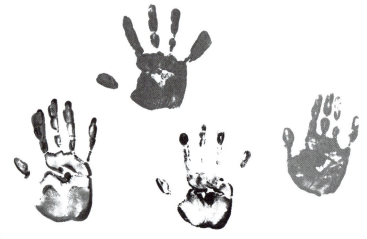

Vocabulary

English: *recommendation;* See *Book Discussion Card* 17, *Charlie Anderson* (Charlie Anderson), for additional words.

Spanish: *recomendación*

Question of the Day: Have you ever seen someone _____? (Name the special skill of today's visitor.)

Large Group

Opening Routine

- Sing a welcome song and talk about who's here.

Chant: "Are You Ready?"

- Use Mighty Minutes 73, "Are You Ready?" Follow the guidance on the card.

Discussion and Shared Writing: Family Member Visit

- Talk about the question of the day.
- Introduce the family member or invite the related child to do the introduction.
- Invite the visitor to describe the skill she can perform.
- Invite children to ask the questions they generated during large-group roundup yesterday.
- Record the visitor's responses.

Before transitioning to interest areas, describe the books about families in the Library area. Show a few of the books and display them in a prominent place for children to notice. Talk about the titles, illustrations, or storylines to get children interested in the books.

Choice Time

As you interact with children in the interest areas, make time to

- Read books with children in the Library area.

> **Reading aloud is the best way to inspire a child's love for reading and promote language and literacy skills.**

Beginning the Year Focus Questions

Read-Aloud

Read *Charlie Anderson*.

- Use Book Discussion Card 17, *Charlie Anderson*. Follow the guidance for the third read-aloud.

Small Group

Option 1: Can You Find It?

- Use Intentional Teaching Card M51, "Can You Find It?"
- Follow the guidance on the card using a collection of common classroom objects.

Option 2: Where Does It Belong?

- Use Intentional Teaching Card M51, "Can You Find It?"
- Follow the guidance on the card using a collection of common classroom objects.

- Take photos of the places where children find the objects and where they store them.
- Make a book using the photos, e.g., "Scissors don't belong in the Block area. Scissors do belong in the Art area."

> **Repeating small-group activities provides opportunities for children to build on recently acquired knowledge.**

Mighty Minutes®

- Use Mighty Minutes 87, "One, Two, Buckle My Shoe." Try the variation on the back of the card.

Large-Group Roundup

- Recall the day's events.
- Write a group thank-you note to the visitor. Invite the children to add drawings to the note and sign their names.
- Invite children who read books in the Library area to talk about those they particularly enjoyed.

- Invite each child who talks about a book to write his or her name on a sticky note and attach it to the first page of the book. Explain, "When you enjoy doing something, you can make a *recommendation* about it to other people. That means you like it so much that you think other people should try it. You may write your name on a sticky note and put it inside a book you like. That is your way of making a book *recommendation*."

| AT A GLANCE | # Focus Question 4 |

When do things happen at school?

Vocabulary—English: *jalapeño, bagel, clock, schedule*

	Day 1	Day 2
Interest Areas	**Music and Movement:** rhythm sticks	**Toys and Games:** interlocking building materials, e.g., LEGO® bricks, star builders, and bristle blocks
Question of the Day	Do you know how this is used? (Display a picture of a clock.)	What do we do after snack? (Offer two choices, e.g., go outside or take a nap.)
Large Group	**Rhyme:** "Hickory Dickory Dock" **Discussion and Shared Writing:** Exploring Beat **Materials:** Mighty Minutes 80, "Hickory Dickory Dock"; real clock or watch; rhythm sticks	**Rhyme:** "Hickory Dickory Dock" **Discussion and Shared Writing:** Our Class Schedule **Materials:** Mighty Minutes 80, "Hickory Dickory Dock"; numeral cards; classroom schedule with words and pictures
Read-Aloud	*Jalapeño Bagels*	*Peeny Butter Fudge*
Small Group	**Option 1: Where's the Beanbag?** Intentional Teaching Card M56, "Where's the Beanbag?"; beanbags; basket or tub; masking tape **Option 2: Stepping Stones** Intentional Teaching Card M55, "Stepping Stones"; masking tape or chalk	**Option 1: Where's the Beanbag?** Intentional Teaching Card M56, "Where's the Beanbag?"; beanbags; basket or tub; masking tape **Option 2: Stepping Stones** Intentional Teaching Card M55, "Stepping Stones"; masking tape or chalk
Mighty Minutes®	Mighty Minutes 93, "Oh, Dear! What Can the Matter Be?"	Mighty Minutes 25, "Freeze"; dance music

Spanish: *jalapeño, bagel, reloj, horario*

Day 3

Discovery: collection of familiar classroom items; magnifying glasses

Technology: eBook version of *Papi, How Many Stars Are in the Sky?*

What do we do when we first get to school? (Offer two choices, e.g., wash hands or take a nap.)

Movement: Let's Make Letters

Discussion and Shared Writing: Cues for Times of the Day

Materials: Mighty Minutes 84, "Let's Make Letters"; *Quinito, Day and Night;* family photos of daily events; familiar classroom item

Materials for Large-Group Roundup: Intentional Teaching Card LL46, "Storyboard"; photos of the children engaged in classroom activities during the day; tape; construction paper; writing tools

Papi, How Many Stars Are in the Sky?

Option 1: The Long and Short of It

Intentional Teaching Card M25, "The Long and Short of It"; container; pieces of ribbon or yarn (one per child)

Option 2: Morning, Noon, and Night

Intentional Teaching Card M60, "Morning, Noon, & Night"; magazines; scissors; chart paper; glue sticks; markers

Mighty Minutes 84, "Let's Make Letters"

Make Time for…

Outdoor Experiences

Physical Fun

- Use Intentional Teaching Card P16, "Body Part Balance." Follow the guidance on the card.

Family Partnerships

- Ask families to bring in pictures of daily home life activities, e.g., preparing a meal, washing dishes, brushing teeth, and reading stories.
- Invite families to access the eBook, *Papi, How Many Stars Are in the Sky?*

Day 1 — Focus Question 4

When do things happen at school?

Vocabulary
English: *jalapeño, bagel, clock*
Spanish: *jalapeño, bagel, reloj*
Question of the Day: Do you know how this is used? (Display a picture of a clock.)

Large Group

Opening Routine
- Sing a welcome song and talk about who's here.

Rhyme: "Hickory Dickory Dock"
- Use Mighty Minutes 80, "Hickory Dickory Dock." Follow the guidance on the card.

> Young children enjoy exploring the tools for telling time. However, they think about time in terms of "chunks" of the day that are related to their experiences, e.g., snack time, rest time, group time, and time to go home. Learning to tell time doesn't typically occur until around age 6 or 7.

Discussion and Shared Writing: Exploring Beat
- Show the children a real clock or watch.
- Talk about the question of the day.
- Explain, "A *clock* is a tool for telling time."
- Have children listen to the ticking of the clock or make the ticking sound yourself. Invite them to move a part of their bodies to the beat.
- Next, invite children to make a steady beat with their hands or feet.
- Introduce rhythm sticks and demonstrate how to use them safely.
- Invite children to use the rhythm sticks to tap a steady beat while singing "Hickory Dickory Dock."
- For children who are ready, consider having them tap the sticks to match the number in the verse. For example, if you say, "The clock struck four," the child taps the sticks four times.

English-language learners
Incorporate children's home languages into daily classroom activities through songs, poetry, dances, rhymes, and counting.

Before transitioning to interest areas, talk about how they may use the rhythm sticks in the Music and Movement area.

Beginning the Year Focus Questions

Choice Time	As you interact with children in the interest areas, make time to • Observe children as they play the rhythm sticks.	• Say a rhyme or encourage children to sing a song while they tap along to the beat.
Read-Aloud	Read *Jalapeño Bagels*. • **Before you read**, show the book cover and read the title. Say, "I wonder what a *jalapeño bagel* is." Ask, "Do you have any guesses about that?" • **As you read**, define *jalapeño* and *bagel*.	• **After you read**, say, "Pablo makes many special foods with his family." Ask, "What special foods do you make with your family?"
Small Group	**Option 1: Where's the Beanbag?** • Use Intentional Teaching Card M56, "Where's the Beanbag?" Follow the guidance on the card. **Option 2: Stepping Stones** • Use Intentional Teaching Card M55, "Stepping Stones." Follow the guidance on the card.	**English-language learners** Teacher-guided small-group activities offer opportunities for all children to get involved and interact with others. For children who have been working in isolation, the small-group structure is a good stepping-stone to participation in a larger group.
Mighty Minutes®	• Use Mighty Minutes 93, "Oh, Dear! What Can the Matter Be?" Follow the guidance on the card.	
Large-Group Roundup	• Recall the day's events. • Repeat the rhythm sticks experience from today's large-group time.	

The Creative Curriculum® for Preschool

Day 2   Focus Question 4

When do things happen at school?

Vocabulary
English: schedule
Spanish: horario
Question of the Day: What do we do after snack?
(Offer two choices, e.g., go outside or take a nap.)

Large Group

Opening Routine

- Sing a welcome song and talk about who's here.

Rhyme: "Hickory Dickory Dock"

- Use Mighty Minutes 80, "Hickory Dickory Dock." Try the numeral card variation on the back of the card.

Discussion and Shared Writing: Our Class Schedule

- Remind children that a clock is a tool used for telling time.

- Introduce the daily classroom schedule (made with words and pictures). Explain, "Looking at our *schedule* is another way to tell time and find out what comes next in our day."

- Read the schedule, briefly talking about the various times of the day.

- Practice having children read the schedule. Talk about the question of the day.

- Say, "Let's pretend we're eating lunch. Let's look at the *schedule* and figure out what comes next."

- Repeat with other activities and times of the day.

Before transitioning to interest areas, talk about the interlocking building materials in the Toys and Games area. Explain how children may use and store them.

English-language learners
Classroom routines help give children a sense of security, which they need to acquire before they can begin to experiment with a new language.

Choice Time

As you interact with children in the interest areas, make time to

- Observe children as they use the interlocking building materials in the Toys and Games area.

- Ask children open-ended questions to encourage conversation about their work, e.g., "What can you tell me about your building?"

- Designate a protected space in the classroom to display children's constructions. Alternatively, consider taking photos of their constructions to display.

Beginning the Year Focus Questions

Read-Aloud

Read *Peeny Butter Fudge.*

- **Before you read**, ask, "What is this story about?"
- **As you read**, point out the schedule that the mother leaves for the grandmother and children to follow.
- **After you read**, review the schedule and ask, "Did the grandmother follow the *schedule*?"

> For more information on supporting children's vocabulary development, see Intentional Teaching Card LL43, "Introducing New Vocabulary."

Small Group

Option 1: Where's the Beanbag?

- Use Intentional Teaching Card M56, "Where's the Beanbag?" Follow the guidance on the card.

Option 2: Stepping Stones

- Use Intentional Teaching Card M55, "Stepping Stones." Follow the guidance on the card.

Mighty Minutes®

- Use Mighty Minutes 25, "Freeze." Follow the guidance on the card.

Large-Group Roundup

- Recall the day's events.
- Invite children who worked with the interlocking building materials during choice time to talk about what they built.

The Creative Curriculum® for Preschool

Day 3 Focus Question 4

When do things happen at school?

Vocabulary
English: *schedule*
Spanish: *horario*
Question of the Day: What do we do when we first get to school? (Offer two choices, e.g., wash hands or take a nap.)

Large Group

Opening Routine

- Sing a welcome song and talk about who's here.

Movement: "Let's Make Letters"

- Use Mighty Minutes 84, "Let's Make Letters." Follow the guidance on the card.

Discussion and Shared Writing: Cues for Times of the Day

- Share photos that families have brought in showing daily events at home.
- Read *Quinito, Day and Night*.
- Show the class schedule again.
- Compare the events in Quinito's day to the events on your class schedule.
- Discuss the cues you give children throughout the day to tell them that it is time to move on to another daily event, e.g., ringing a bell on the playground to signal that it is time to go inside or playing a chime to give a 5-minute warning before cleanup time.

English-language learners
Introducing books to English-language learners in their home languages before they are read aloud in English supports their comprehension of the stories. Encourage Spanish-speaking children to listen to the Spanish eBooks before they are read aloud.

Before transitioning to interest areas, show a familiar classroom item and ask, "What is this? How do we use it?" Then ask, "How else could we use it?" Invite children to explore the collection of items in the Discovery area during choice time.

Choice Time

As you interact with children in the interest areas, make time to

- Talk to the children about the items in the Discovery area.
- Invite children to think creatively about new ways to use the items.
- Record their ideas about the new uses.

Beginning the Year Focus Questions

Read-Aloud

Read *Papi, How Many Stars Are in the Sky?*

- **Before you read**, show the book cover and read the title. Ask, "How many stars do you think are in the sky?"
- **As you read**, pause to answer children's questions about the story. Explain any words that children may not understand.

- **After you read**, say, "At the end of the story, the grandfather sang to the children in Spanish. What songs do you know in a language other than English?" Tell the children the book will be available to them on the computer in the Technology area.

Small Group

Option 1: The Long and Short of It

- Use Intentional Teaching Card M25, "The Long and Short of It." Follow the guidance on the card.

Option 2: Morning, Noon, and Night

- Use Intentional Teaching Card M60, "Morning, Noon, and Night." Follow the guidance on the card.
- Talk about the question of the day.
- Remind the children about Quinito in *Quinito, Day and Night*.
- Explain, "Quinito did different things at different times of the day."

Mighty Minutes®

- Use Mighty Minutes 84, "Let's Make Letters." Follow the guidance on the card.

Large-Group Roundup

- Recall the day's events.
- Show photos of the children engaged in classroom activities during various times of the day.

- Use Intentional Teaching Card LL46, "Storyboard." Follow the guidance on the card using the photos to create a story.

AT A GLANCE

Focus Question 5

Who works at our school?

Vocabulary—English: *neighborhood*

	Day 1	Day 2	Day 3
Interest Areas	**Music and Movement:** beanbags **Technology:** eBook version of *The Gingerbread Man*	**Cooking:** equipment, ingredients for selected recipe (Select an *Intentional Teaching Card* recipe, or ask a family member to bring one.) **Technology:** eBook version of *Neighborhood Song*	**Sand and Water:** measuring cups; measuring spoons; mixing spoons; whisks **Technology:** eBook version of *The Gingerbread Man*
Question of the Day	Does this person work at our school? (Display a picture of a school worker or a character who does not work at school, such as a clown.)	Have you seen this person at our school? (Display a picture of a school worker.)	Does this man go to our school? (Display a picture of the Gingerbread Man.)
Large Group	**Song:** "Hello Bingo" **Discussion and Shared Writing:** Who Do You Think Works at Our School? **Materials:** Mighty Minutes 77, "Hello Bingo"; *Kevin and His Dad*	**Game:** Busy Bees **Discussion and Shared Writing:** Visit From a School Worker **Materials:** Mighty Minutes 75, "Busy Bees"; Mighty Minutes 31, "What's Inside the Box?"; box; tools the visitor uses in his or her job	**Song:** "Let's Clean Up!" **Discussion and Shared Writing:** Visit From a School Worker **Materials:** Mighty Minutes 82, "Let's Clean Up!"; Mighty Minutes 31, "What's Inside the Box?"; box; tools the visitor uses in her job **Materials for Large-Group Roundup:** a gingerbread man
Read-Aloud	*The Gingerbread Man* Book Discussion Card 13 (first read-aloud)	*Neighborhood Song*	*The Gingerbread Man* Book Discussion Card 13 (second read-aloud)
Small Group	**Option 1: Geoboards** Intentional Teaching Card M21, "Geoboards"; geoboards; geobands; shape cards with one shape on each **Option 2: Missing Lids** Intentional Teaching Card M58, "Missing Lids"; containers with lids of various sizes and shapes	**Option 1: Alphabet Cards** Intentional Teaching Card LL03, "Alphabet Cards"; alphabet cards; manipulatives **Option 2:** *D Is for Door* Intentional Teaching Card LL48, "*D Is for Door*"; alphabet cards; tape	**Option 1: Alphabet Cards** Intentional Teaching Card LL03, "Alphabet Cards"; alphabet cards; manipulatives **Option 2:** *D Is for Door* Intentional Teaching Card LL48, "*D Is for Door*"; alphabet cards; tape
Mighty Minutes®	Mighty Minutes 85, "Listen for Your Name"	Mighty Minutes 58, "A-Hunting We Will Go"	Mighty Minutes 82, "Let's Clean Up!"

Spanish: *vecindario*

Day 4	Make Time for…

Toys and Games: magnetic letters

Technology: eBook version of *Neighborhood Song*

Outdoor Experiences

Physical Fun

- Use Intentional Teaching Card P11, "Jump the River." Follow the guidance on the card.

Family Partnerships

- Invite a family member to visit the classroom on day 2 and cook with the children. You may select one of the *Intentional Teaching Card* recipes for the guest to use, or invite the visitor to bring his own recipe and ingredients.
- Invite families to access the eBook, *Neighborhood Song*.

What does this person do at our school? (Display a picture of a school helper and offer a choice between two jobs.)

Movement: Oh, Dear! What Can the Matter Be?

Discussion and Shared Writing: The Missing Gingerbread Man

Materials: Mighty Minutes 93, "Oh, Dear! What Can the Matter Be?"; note from the Gingerbread Man

Wow! Experiences

- Day 2: Visit from a school worker whose job relates to food preparation or delivery
- Day 2: Visit from a family member to cook during choice time
- Day 3: Visit from a school worker whose job relates to maintaining the school, keeping it clean, or both

Neighborhood Song

Option 1: Gingerbread

Intentional Teaching Card M54, "Gingerbread Cookies" (See card for equipment, ingredients, and recipe.)

Option 2: Modeling Clay

Intentional Teaching Card M52, "Modeling Clay" (See card for equipment, ingredients, and recipe.)

Mighty Minutes 01, "The People in Your Neighborhood"

Day 1 Focus Question 5

Who works at our school?

Vocabulary

English: See Book Discussion Card 13, *The Gingerbread Man* (*El hombrecito de jengibre*), for words.

Question of the Day: Does this person work at our school? (Display a picture of a school worker or a character who does not work at school, such as a clown.)

Large Group

English-language learners
Use role plays and pantomimes to help children learn new vocabulary. These techniques, effective for all children, are particularly helpful for English-language learners.

Opening Routine

- Sing a welcome song and talk about who's here.

Song: "Hello Bingo"

- Use Mighty Minutes 77, "Hello Bingo." Follow the guidance on the card.
- Write *Hello* in big letters, and point to the letters as you sing.

Discussion and Shared Writing: Who Do You Think Works at Our School?

- Read *Kevin and His Dad*.
- Using examples from the story, talk about the ways in which family members help each other at home.
- Explain, "Just like family members help each other at home, we help each other at school. There are special people here at our school who help to prepare our food and keep our school clean."
- Talk about the question of the day.
- Say, "Tomorrow we're having a visitor. It's someone who helps at our school."
- Give clues and invite the children to guess the person's job.
- After the children have identified who is coming, ask, "What would you like to ask our visitor tomorrow? I want to ask, 'Do you have to wear special clothes for your job?'" When you model ways to ask questions, children learn that the classroom is a good place to wonder, question, and seek answers.
- Record children's responses.

Before transitioning to interest areas, talk about the beanbags in the Music and Movement area and how children can use them to try balancing bean bags on different parts of their bodies.

Beginning the Year Focus Questions

Choice Time

As you interact with children in the interest areas, make time to

- Invite children to try balancing beanbags on different parts of their bodies while they move in a variety of ways, e.g., balancing a beanbag on their heads while jumping, on their backs while crawling, and on their knees while crab walking.

- Take pictures of the children balancing the bean bags.

Read-Aloud

- Read *The Gingerbread Man*.
- Review Book Discussion Card 13, *The Gingerbread Man*. Follow the guidance for the first read-aloud.

- Tell the children that the book will be available to them on the computer in the Technology area.

Small Group

Option 1: Geoboards

- Use Intentional Teaching Card M21, "Geoboards." Follow the guidance on the card.

Option 2: Missing Lids

- Use Intentional Teaching Card M58, "Missing Lids." Follow the guidance on the card.

English-language learners
When pairing children for an activity, consider establishing a system in which English-speaking children "buddy" with English-language learners. Select partners who can help each other feel comfortable and successful.

Mighty Minutes®

- Use Mighty Minutes 85, "Listen for Your Name." Follow the guidance on the card.

Large-Group Roundup

- Recall the day's events.
- Invite children who balanced beanbags during choice time to share what they discovered.
- Tell children about the two visitors who will be visiting the classroom tomorrow.

Day 2 — Focus Question 5

Who works at our school?

Vocabulary
English: neighborhood
Spanish: vecindario
Question of the Day: Have you seen this person at our school? (Display a picture of a school worker.)

Large Group

Opening Routine
- Sing a welcome song and talk about who's here.

Game: Busy Bees
- Use Mighty Minutes 75, "Busy Bees." Follow the guidance on the card.

Discussion and Shared Writing: Visit From a School Worker
- Talk about the question of the day.
- Review Mighty Minutes 31, "What's Inside the Box?"
- Follow the guidance on the card using tools that the visiting school worker uses in his job.
- Introduce the visitor and invite him to talk to the children about his job.
- Invite children to ask the questions they generated yesterday.
- Record the visitor's responses.

> **Take pictures of each school worker as the children learn about them. Create a display or chart with the pictures and the school workers' names and titles.**

Before transitioning to interest areas, talk about the recipe that the children may help prepare with the visiting family member in the Cooking area.

Choice Time

As you interact with children in the interest areas, make time to
- Help children use the recipe in the Cooking area.
- If you're using an *Intentional Teaching Card*, follow the guidance on the card that you selected.

> **Classroom volunteers may feel very comfortable with cooking activities. Having an extra set of hands in the Cooking area at the beginning of the year frees you to be more responsive to the children who are involved in other activities.**

Beginning the Year Focus Questions

Read-Aloud

Read *Neighborhood Song*.

- **Before you read**, show the book cover and read the title. Ask, "What is a *neighborhood*?"
- **As you read**, sing the words in the book to the tune of the "Here We Go Round the Mulberry Bush."
- **After you read**, ask, "What kinds of things do you do in your *neighborhood*?" Tell the children that the book will be available to them on the computer in the Technology area.

Small Group

Option 1: Alphabet Cards

- Use Intentional Teaching Card LL03, "Alphabet Cards." Follow the guidance on the card.

Option 2: *D* is for *Door*

- Use Intentional Teaching Card LL48, "*D* Is for *Door*." Follow the guidance on the card.

Mighty Minutes®

- Use Mighty Minutes 58, "A-Hunting We Will Go." Follow the guidance on the card.

Large-Group Roundup

- Recall the day's events.
- Tell the children that another school worker will be visiting the class tomorrow. Explain the person's job at the school.
- Ask, "What would you like to ask our visitor tomorrow?"
- Record children's questions.

English-language learners
It is common for children to stop speaking their home languages for a time and become nonverbal when they realize that others don't understand them. This behavior does not indicate a lack of abilities or an unwillingness to participate. During this nonverbal period, children use facial expressions, body movements, and gestures to communicate.

The Creative Curriculum® for Preschool

Day 3 — Focus Question 5

Who works at our school?

Vocabulary

English: See *Book Discussion Card* 13, *The Gingerbread Man* (*El hombrecito de jengibre*), for words.

Question of the Day: Does this man go to our school? (Display a picture of the Gingerbread Man.)

Large Group

Opening Routine

- Sing a welcome song and talk about who's here.

Song: "Let's Clean Up!"

- Use Mighty Minutes 82, "Let's Clean Up!" Follow the guidance on the card.

Discussion and Shared Writing: Visit From a School Worker

- Review Mighty Minutes 31, "What's Inside the Box?"
- Follow the guidance on the card using tools the school worker uses in her job.
- Introduce the school worker, and invite the visitor to talk to the children about her job.
- Invite children to ask the questions they generated yesterday.
- Record the visitor's responses.

Before transitioning to interest areas, talk about the tools in the Sand and Water area and how children may use them.

Choice Time

As you interact with children in the interest areas, make time to

- Observe children as they use the cooking tools in the Sand and Water area.
- Ask questions to encourage children to explore the materials and explain their process, e.g., "What happened when you mixed the sand with the whisk? How many cups do you think it will it take to fill that container?"

Beginning the Year Focus Questions

Read-Aloud

Read *The Gingerbread Man*.

- Use Book Discussion Card 13, *The Gingerbread Man*. Follow the guidance for the second read-aloud.

Small Group

Option 1: Alphabet Cards

- Use Intentional Teaching Card LL03, "Alphabet Cards." Follow the guidance on the card.

Option 2: *D* Is for *Door*

- Use Intentional Teaching Card LL48, "*D* Is for *Door*." Follow the guidance on the card.

Mighty Minutes®

- Use Mighty Minutes 82, "Let's Clean Up!" Follow the guidance on the card.

Large-Group Roundup

- Recall the day's events.
- Write a group thank-you note to the visitors who came yesterday and today. Invite the children to add drawings to the note and sign their names.
- Talk about the question of the day.
- Show the children a gingerbread man, which can be made from dough or art materials.
- Explain, "This is the Gingerbread Man, like the one in our story. He's our new friend, and he came to see us in our classroom. But we're going to leave him here tonight, and we'll visit with him tomorrow. Let's put him in a chair so he can join our group in the morning."

> **Before large-group time tomorrow, give the Gingerbread Man to someone who works in the school. Ask that person to create a playful story about catching the Gingerbread Man. Leave a note on the chair where the children last saw him that says, "Run, run, as fast as you can. You can't catch me. I'm the Gingerbread Man!" You will lead the children on a walk around the school, meeting school workers while you look for your missing Gingerbread Man.**

The Creative Curriculum® for Preschool

Day 4 Focus Question 5

Who works at our school?

Vocabulary

English: *neighborhood*

Spanish: *vecindario*

Question of the Day: What does this person do at our school? (Display a picture of a school helper and offer a choice between two jobs.)

Large Group

Opening Routine

- Sing a welcome song and talk about who's here.

Movement: Oh, Dear! What Can the Matter Be?

- Use Mighty Minutes 93, "Oh, Dear! What Can the Matter Be?" Follow the guidance on the card.

> Children love intrigue and make-believe. Imaginary thinking helps them make sense of their experiences and try new ways to solve problems. Remember always to follow up such experiences by asking, "Was this real, or was it pretend?" That helps children think about the difference.

> Before the walk, make sure you have already given the Gingerbread Man to the last person the children will meet on the walk and that he or she is prepared to tell the children about how the Gingerbread Man was caught.

Discussion and Shared Writing: The Missing Gingerbread Man

- Show the children the spot where you placed the Gingerbread Man yesterday, and call attention to the note that was left in his chair. Read the note together: "Run, run as fast as you can. You can't catch me. I'm the Gingerbread Man!"

- Exclaim, "He's missing! I wonder where he went."

- Ask, "Where do you think he went?"

- Say, "Let's walk around the school. We can ask people we meet whether they have any clues about our missing Gingerbread Man."

Before transitioning to interest areas, talk about the magnetic letters in the Toys and Games area and how children may use them.

Beginning the Year Focus Questions

Choice Time	As you interact with children in the interest areas, make time to • Observe children as they play with the magnetic letters in the Toys and Games area.	• Pay attention to what letters and letter sounds they know.
Read-Aloud	Read *Neighborhood Song*. • **Before you read**, ask, "What is this book about?" • **As you read**, invite children to sing along.	• **After you read**, look through the book with the children. Ask, "What kinds of things do people do in their *neighborhoods* that we also do in school?" Tell the children that the book will be available to them on the computer in the Technology area.
Small Group	**Option 1: Gingerbread Cookies** • Use Intentional Teaching Card M54, "Gingerbread Cookies." Follow the guidance on the card.	**Option 2: Modeling Clay** • Use Intentional Teaching Card M52, "Modeling Clay." Follow the guidance on the card.
Mighty Minutes®	• Use Mighty Minutes 01, "The People in Your Neighborhood." Follow the guidance on the card using the people the children visited around the school.	
Large-Group Roundup	• Recall the day's events. • Talk about the question of the day.	• Lead a discussion about all the people the children met on their walk around the school.

The Creative Curriculum® for Preschool

AT A GLANCE

Focus Question 6

How do we make and keep friends? How can we be part of a group?

Vocabulary—English: *take turns, piñata, friends, microphone*

	Day 1	Day 2	Day 3
Interest Areas	**Toys and Games:** geoboards; geobands **Technology:** eBook version of *The Gingerbread Man*	**Blocks:** variety of block shapes	**Library:** materials for making cards
Question of the Day	Can you make this shape with your hands? (Display a picture of a triangle.)	Do you know what this is? (Display a picture of a piñata.)	What do you like to do with your friends? (Provide sticky notes for children to draw on.)
Large Group	**Song:** "Hello Friends" **Discussion and Shared Writing:** Taking Turns **Materials:** Mighty Minutes 78, "Hello Friends"; Intentional Teaching Card P22, "Follow the Leader"; toy truck	**Game:** Name Cheer **Discussion and Shared Writing:** Friendship **Materials:** Mighty Minutes 92, "Name Cheer"; letter cards; *The Adventures of Gary & Harry;* several unit blocks of different shapes	**Rhyme:** "The Name Dance" **Discussion and Shared Writing:** Friendship **Materials:** Mighty Minutes 60, "The Name Dance"; Intentional Teaching Card SE19, "Friendship & Love Cards"
Read-Aloud	*The Gingerbread Man* Book Discussion Card 13 (third read-aloud)	*Hooray, a Piñata!*	*Too Many Tamales* Book Discussion Card 21 (first read-aloud)
Small Group	**Option 1: Bookmaking** Intentional Teaching Card LL04, "Bookmaking"; cardboard or card stock; paper; pencils, crayons, or markers; bookbinding supplies **Option 2: Desktop Publishing** Intentional Teaching Card LL02, "Desktop Publishing"; digital camera; computer; each child's word bank; printer; paper; bookbinding supplies	**Option 1: Bookmaking** Intentional Teaching Card LL04, "Bookmaking"; cardboard or card stock; paper; pencils, crayons, or markers; bookbinding supplies **Option 2: Desktop Publishing** Intentional Teaching Card LL02, "Desktop Publishing"; digital camera; computer; each child's word bank; printer; paper; bookbinding supplies	**Option 1: Bookmaking** Intentional Teaching Card LL04, "Bookmaking"; cardboard or card stock; paper; pencils, crayons, or markers; bookbinding supplies **Option 2: Desktop Publishing** Intentional Teaching Card LL02, "Desktop Publishing"; digital camera; computer; each child's word bank; printer; paper; bookbinding supplies
Mighty Minutes®	Mighty Minutes 96, "This Old Man"	Mighty Minutes 42, "Come Play With Me"	Mighty Minutes 96, "This Old Man"

Spanish: *turnarse, piñata, amigos, micrófono*

Day 4	Day 5	Make Time for…
Library: books about friends **Technology:** eBook version of *Crazy Pizza Day*	**Art:** play dough	### Outdoor Experiences **Physical Fun** • Use Intentional Teaching Card P22, "Follow the Leader." Follow the guidance on the card. • Emphasize taking turns at being the leader.
Which book would you like to read today? (Display two books about friendship.)	What should you do if you and a friend want the same toy? (Scream or take turns.)	### Family Partnerships • Invite family members to accompany the group on the walk around the school next week. • Invite families to access the eBooks, *The Gingerbread Man* and *Crazy Pizza Day*.
Movement: Move to the Beat **Discussion and Shared Writing:** Our Class Book **Materials:** Mighty Minutes 91, "Move to the Beat"; drum; Mighty Minutes 42, "Come Play With Me"; class book	**Game:** Sorting Syllables **Discussion and Shared Writing:** Conflict Resolution **Materials:** Mighty Minutes 95, "Sorting Syllables"; three hula hoops; numerals *1, 2, 3*; Intentional Teaching Card SE08, "Group Problem Solving"	**English-language learners** Playing "Follow the Leader" is a good way to encourage all children to participate as leaders in the classroom. The activity does not require a strong English vocabulary.
Crazy Pizza Day	*Too Many Tamales* Book Discussion Card 21 (second read-aloud)	
Option 1: My Turn at the Microphone Intentional Teaching Card SE10, "My Turn at the Microphone"; real or pretend microphone **Option 2: Recording My Turn at the Microphone** Intentional Teaching Card SE10, "My Turn at the Microphone"; real or pretend microphone; video camera or sound recording device	**Option 1: Nursery Rhyme Count** Intentional Teaching Card M13, "Nursery Rhyme Count"; cotton balls or white pompoms; green construction paper; numeral cards **Option 2: Bounce & Count** Intentional Teaching Card M18, "Bounce & Count"; a variety of balls that bounce	
Mighty Minutes 25, "Freeze"; dance music	Mighty Minutes 42, "Come Play With Me"	

Day 1   Focus Question 6

How do we make and keep friends? How can we be part of a group?

Vocabulary

English: *take turns;* See *Book Discussion Card* 13, *The Gingerbread Man* (*El hombrecito de jengibre*), for additional words.

Spanish: *turnarse*

Question of the Day: Can you make this shape with your hands? (Display a picture of a triangle.)

Large Group

Opening Routine

- Sing a welcome song and talk about who's here.

Song: "Hello Friends"

- Use Mighty Minutes 78, "Hello Friends." Follow the guidance on the card.

English-language learners
Observe English-language learners carefully when the class sings in unison. Children who have not yet begun to
use English around others often begin using it when singing in a group.

Discussion and Shared Writing: Taking Turns

- Use Intentional Teaching Card P22, "Follow the Leader." Follow the guidance on the card.
- After both partners have had a turn to be leader, explain, "You *took turns* being the leader in that game."
- Ask, "What does *take turns* mean?"
- Discuss children's responses.
- Say, "Let's pretend I'm playing with this truck and you want a *turn*. What can you do to let me know you would like to have a *turn*?"
- Record children's responses. Discuss responses that do not support classroom rules and redirect the conversation. For example say, "Sometimes children grab things from other people when they want a *turn*. One of our rules is "Be kind to others." Grabbing is not kind. What is a kind way to let someone know that you'd like a *turn*?"

English-language learners
Make sure that children understand the idiom *take turns*. Most young children are literal thinkers, so they may misunderstand the meaning of the phrase. Even English-language learners who are familiar with the concept of taking turns might not have heard this common English expression.

> Three- and 4-year-olds are just learning to share. When children struggle with sharing, use the conflict as an opportunity to teach and solve problems together. Say, "What can we do so you both have a turn?"

Before transitioning to interest areas, review the question of the day. Talk about the geoboards in the Toys and Games area and how children may use them.

Beginning the Year Focus Questions

Choice Time	As you interact with children in the interest areas, make time to • Observe how children use the geoboards. • Listen for the words they use to describe the shapes they create.	• Ask questions to encourage them to think about shapes, e.g., "How can you make your triangle bigger?" • Invite children to save their designed geoboards to share during large-group roundup today.
Read-Aloud	Read *The Gingerbread Man*. • Use Book Discussion Card 13, *The Gingerbread Man*. Follow the guidance for the third read-aloud.	• Tell the children that the book will be available to them on the computer in the Technology area.
Small Group	**Option 1: Bookmaking** • Use Intentional Teaching Card LL04, "Bookmaking." Follow the guidance on the card. • Invite children to create a book about things the class likes to do together at school.	**Option 2: Desktop Publishing** • Use Intentional Teaching Card LL02, "Desktop Publishing." Follow the guidance on the card. • Invite children to create a book about things the class likes to do together at school. **Providing a digital camera for children to take their own pictures gives them more ownership over the bookmaking process.**
Mighty Minutes®	• Use Mighty Minutes 96, "This Old Man." Follow the guidance on the card.	
Large-Group Roundup	• Recall the day's events. • Invite children who worked with geoboards during choice time to share their creations with the group. Encourage children to use shape words to describe their work.	

The Creative Curriculum® for Preschool

Day 2 Focus Question 6

How do we make and keep friends? How can we be part of a group?

Vocabulary
English: *piñata, friends*
Spanish: *piñata, amigos*
Question of the Day: Do you know what this is? (Display a picture of a piñata.)

Large Group

Opening Routine

- Sing a welcome song and talk about who's here.

Game: "Name Cheer"

- Use Mighty Minutes 92, "Name Cheer." Follow the guidance on the card.

Discussion and Shared Writing: Friendship

- Read *The Adventures of Gary & Harry*.
- Ask, "How do you know that Gary and Harry were *friends*? What did they do to show that they were *friends*?"
- Record children's responses.

> For more information on supporting children to interact with peers and make friends, see *Volume 6: Objectives for Development & Learning*, Objective 2.

Before transitioning to interest areas, show a few unit blocks of different shapes. Ask, "What shapes do you see when you look at this block? How is this block similar to that one? How are they different?" Invite children to build with a variety of block shapes during choice time.

Choice Time

As you interact with children in the interest areas, make time to

- Talk with children about the structures they build in the Block area. Ask, "What can you tell me about the structure you built?"
- Have conversations with individual children about what they like to do with their friends.

Beginning the Year Focus Questions

Read-Aloud

Read *Hooray, a Piñata!*

- **Before you read**, talk about the question of the day.
- **As you read**, point out where Lucky is in the illustrations. Explain, "Samson was such a good *friend* to get Clara another *piñata* for her party. Friends do nice things for each other."
- **After you read**, invite children to talk about their experiences with piñatas.

Small Group

Option 1: Bookmaking

- Use Intentional Teaching Card LL04, "Bookmaking." Follow the guidance on the card.
- Invite children to create a book about things the class likes to do together at school.

Option 2: Desktop Publishing

- Use Intentional Teaching Card LL02, "Desktop Publishing." Follow the guidance on the card
- Invite children to create a book about things the class likes to do together at school.

Mighty Minutes®

- Use Mighty Minutes 42, "Come Play With Me." Follow the guidance on the card.

Large-Group Roundup

- Recall the day's events.
- Invite children to talk about their experiences building in the Block area.

Day 3 — Focus Question 6

How do we make and keep friends? How can we be part of a group?

Vocabulary

English: See *Book Discussion Card 21, Too Many Tamales* (*¡Qué montón de tamales!*), for words.

Question of the Day: What do you like to do with your friends? (Provide sticky notes for children to draw on.)

Large Group

Opening Routine
- Sing a welcome song and talk about who's here.

Rhyme: "The Name Dance"
- Use Mighty Minutes 60, "The Name Dance." Follow the guidance on the card.

Discussion and Shared Writing: Friendship
- Recall the friendship between Gary and Harry (from yesterday's discussion during large-group time) and between Clara and Samson (from yesterday's read-aloud).
- Remind children about the things the pairs of friends liked to do together.
- Talk about the question of the day.
- Ask, "What do you like to do with your friends?"
- Record children's responses.

Before transitioning to interest areas, talk about the materials in the Library area and how children may use them to make a card for a friend.

> See Intentional Teaching Card SE19, "Friendship & Love Cards," for more information.

Choice Time

As you interact with children in the interest areas, make time to
- Talk with children about their work in the Library area.
- Record their dictation on their cards when asked.
- Invite children to talk about the friend for whom they are making a card.

Beginning the Year Focus Questions

Read-Aloud

Read *Too Many Tamales*.

- Use Book Discussion Card 21, *Too Many Tamales*. Follow the guidance for the first read-aloud.

Small Group

Option 1: Bookmaking

- Use Intentional Teaching Card LL04, "Bookmaking." Follow the guidance on the card.
- Invite children to create a book about things the class likes to do together at school.

Option 2: Desktop Publishing

- Use Intentional Teaching Card LL02, "Desktop Publishing." Follow the guidance on the card.
- Invite children to create a book about things the class likes to do together at school.

Mighty Minutes®

- Use Mighty Minutes 96, "This Old Man." Follow the guidance on the card.

English-language learners
This is a good opportunity to count in children's home languages as well as in English. This activity helps English-language learners feel included and exposes other children to new languages.

Large-Group Roundup

- Recall the day's events.
- Invite children who made cards in the Library area to share their work.

The Creative Curriculum® for Preschool

Day 4   Focus Question 6

How do we make and keep friends? How can we be part of a group?

Vocabulary

English: *microphone*

Spanish: *micrófono*

Question of the Day: Which book would you like to read today? (Display two books about friendship.)

Large Group

Opening Routine

- Sing a welcome song and talk about who's here.

Movement: Move to the Beat

- Use Mighty Minutes 91, "Move to the Beat." Follow the guidance on the card.

Discussion and Shared Writing: Our Class Book

- Use Mighty Minutes 42, "Come Play With Me." Follow the guidance on the card.
- While counting the children who join and leave the tree, record the numeral as you and the children say it.
- Explain, "Climbing in trees with friends sounds like a lot of fun."
- Say, "Let's read the book we made about what you like to do with your friends at school."
- Read the book that the children created during small-group time over the last few days.
- Invite children to read the pages they created.

Before transitioning to interest areas, discuss the books about friends in the Library area and how children may use them. Review the question of the day. Invite children who are interested to join you in the Library area to listen to the story that the children chose when they answered the question of the day.

Choice Time

As you interact with children in the interest areas, make time to

- Read books about friends with children in the Library area.
- Invite children to relate the stories to their own experiences with friendship.

Beginning the Year Focus Questions

Read-Aloud

Read *Crazy Pizza Day*.

- **Before you read**, say, "I wonder what a 'crazy pizza day' is."
- **As you read**, invite children to comment on the pizzas in the story.
- **After you read**, ask, "Which pizza did you like best? Why?" Tell children that the book will be available to them on the computer in the Technology area.

Small Group

Option 1: My Turn at the Microphone

- Use Intentional Teaching Card SE10, "My Turn at the Microphone." Follow the guidance on the card.

Option 2: Recording My Turn at the Microphone

- Use Intentional Teaching Card SE10, "My Turn at the Microphone." Follow the guidance on the card.
- As children take their turns at the microphone, record their voices to play back later.

Mighty Minutes®

- Use Mighty Minutes 25, "Freeze." Follow the guidance on the card.

Large-Group Roundup

- Recall the day's events.
- Invite children who looked at books about friends in the Library area to talk about a story they enjoyed reading.

The Creative Curriculum® for Preschool

Day 5 — Focus Question 6

How do we make and keep friends? How can we be part of a group?

Vocabulary

English: See *Book Discussion Card 21, Too Many Tamales* (*¡Qué montón de tamales!*), for words.

Question of the Day: What should you do if you and a friend want the same toy? (Scream or take turns.)

Large Group

Opening Routine

- Sing a welcome song and talk about who's here.

Game: Sorting Syllables

- Use Mighty Minutes 95, "Sorting Syllables." Follow the guidance on the card.

> **Helping children attend to smaller and smaller units of sound builds children's phonological awareness. Over time, children will learn that ideas are expressed in sentences. Sentences are made up of individual words. Words can be broken down into syllables and phonemes. These sounds can be put together in different ways to form words that have meaning.**

Discussion and Shared Writing: Conflict Resolution

- Review Intentional Teaching Card SE08, "Group Problem Solving."
- Discuss the question of the day.
- Think of a problem in the classroom that needs the group's attention, e.g., the Block area is not being cleaned up or children have to wait a long time to use the computer.
- Follow the guidance on the card.

Before transitioning to interest areas, talk about the play dough in the Art area and how children may use it.

Beginning the Year Focus Questions

Choice Time

As you interact with children in the interest areas, make time to

- Coach individual children on how to approach a group of children who are already playing.
- Show children how to establish contact by smiling, asking questions, offering ideas, making positive comments, and offering to share something.

> Working with play dough and clay strengthens the small muscles in children's hands—muscles that they need to use for writing.

Read-Aloud

Read *Too Many Tamales*.

- Use Book Discussion Card 21, *Too Many Tamales*. Follow the guidance for the second read-aloud.

Small Group

Option 1: Nursery Rhyme Count

- Use Intentional Teaching Card M13, "Nursery Rhyme Count." Follow the guidance on the card.

Option 2: Bounce & Count

- Use Intentional Teaching Card M18, "Bounce & Count." Follow the guidance on the card.

Mighty Minutes®

- Use Mighty Minutes 42, "Come Play With Me." Follow the guidance on the card.

Large-Group Roundup

- Recall the day's events.
- Invite children to talk about what they made with play dough during choice time.

The Creative Curriculum® for Preschool

Ministudy

AT A GLANCE Ministudy

What sounds do we hear at school? Where do they come from?

Vocabulary—English: *sounds, texture, mystery, interview, observe, remember*

	Day 1	Day 2	Day 3
Interest Areas	**Sand and Water:** variety of glass containers; food coloring; measuring cups; funnel; spoon; Intentional Teaching Card M44, "Musical Water" **Technology:** eBook version of *Rice Is Nice*	**Discovery:** textured materials used to make sounds, e.g., crinkly paper or corrugated cardboard	**Music and Movement:** a variety of bells (or other musical instruments) **Technology:** eBook version of *Crazy Pizza Day*
Question of the Day	Do you know what sound this makes? (Show an item from the classroom or school that makes a sound.)	Which one do you think makes a louder sound? (Display two pictures, e.g., a baby crying and a racing fire engine.)	Does this make a sound? (Display a picture of an animal or a familiar item.)
Large Group	**Song:** "La, La, La" **Discussion and Shared Writing:** What Are the Sounds We Hear Around School? **Materials:** Mighty Minutes 100, "La, La, La"; large piece of cardboard or cloth; objects that make classroom sounds	**Game:** Listening Story **Discussion and Shared Writing:** Choosing Sounds to Investigate **Materials:** Mighty Minutes 86, "Listening Story"	**Rhyme:** "Here Is the Beehive" **Discussion and Shared Writing:** Investigating Sounds **Materials:** Mighty Minutes 79, "Here Is the Beehive"; audio recorder
Read-Aloud	*Rice Is Nice*	*Too Many Tamales* (third read-aloud)	*Crazy Pizza Day* Paper and markers for drawing crazy pizzas
Small Group	**Option 1: Letters, Letters, Letters** Intentional Teaching Card LL07, "Letters, Letters, Letters"; alphabet rubber stamps; colored inkpads; construction paper or magnetic letters and board **Option 2: Shaving Cream Letters** Intentional Teaching Card LL13, "Shaving Cream Letters"; shaving cream; art smocks	**Option 1: Letters, Letters, Letters** Intentional Teaching Card LL07, "Letters, Letters, Letters"; alphabet rubber stamps; colored inkpads; construction paper or magnetic letters and board **Option 2: Shaving Cream Letters** Intentional Teaching Card LL13, "Shaving Cream Letters"; shaving cream; art smocks	**Option 1: Dinnertime** Intentional Teaching Card M01, "Dinnertime"; paper or plastic dishes; napkins; utensils; cups; placemats **Option 2: Let's Go Fishing** Intentional Teaching Card M39, "Let's Go Fishing"; stick or dowel; string; magnet; set of fish cards; paper clips
Mighty Minutes®	Mighty Minutes 13, "Simon Says"	Mighty Minutes 76, "Describing Things"; interesting item; bag	Mighty Minutes 02, "Just Like Mine"

Spanish: *sonidos, textura, misterio, entrevista, observar, recordar*

Day 4	Day 5	Make Time for…
Technology: headphones and interesting sound clips; eBook version of *The Gingerbread Man*	**Music and Movement:** materials, such as empty containers, that can be used as instruments **Technology:** eBook version of *A World of Families*	**Outdoor Experiences** **Physical Fun** • Use Intentional Teaching Card P14, "Moving Through the Forest." Follow the guidance on the card.
Does this make a sound? (Display a picture of an animal or a familiar item.)	Can we make sounds with this? (Display an empty container.)	**Family Partnerships** • Invite family members to join the class on a walk around the school on days 1 and 4 of this week. • Invite families to access the eBook, *Rice Is Nice*.
Song: "La, La, La" **Discussion and Shared Writing:** Investigating Sounds **Materials:** Mighty Minutes 100, "La, La, La"; Intentional Teaching Card LL45, "Observational Drawing"; clipboards with paper; felt-tip pens; musical instruments	**Music:** "Echo Clapping" **Discussion and Shared Writing:** Celebrating Our Learning **Materials:** Mighty Minutes 26, "Echo Clapping"; drums or rhythm sticks; empty containers; classroom items that can be used to produce sounds	**Wow! Experiences** • Day 1: Site visit to explore sounds around the school • Day 3: Interview with someone who knows about one of the sounds heard on day 1 • Day 4: Site visit to investigate the source of one of the sounds heard on day 1
The Gingerbread Man	*A World of Families*	**English-language learners** Research shows that English-language learners who have strong literacy skills in their home languages do better in school than those children who have less proficiency in their home languages. Therefore, encourage families to continue speaking to their children in their home languages to build vocabulary, understanding of new concepts, and conversational skills.
Option 1: Dramatic Story Retelling Intentional Teaching Card LL06, "Dramatic Story Retelling"; *The Gingerbread Man*; story props **Option 2: Clothesline Storytelling** Intentional Teaching Card LL33, "Clothesline Storytelling"; *The Gingerbread Man*; lamination supplies or clear adhesive paper; 6 feet of clothesline; clothespins; a paper star; paper; markers; large resealable bag	**Option 1: Dramatic Story Retelling** Intentional Teaching Card LL06, "Dramatic Story Retelling"; *The Gingerbread Man*; story props **Option 2: Clothesline Storytelling** Intentional Teaching Card LL33, "Clothesline Storytelling"; *The Gingerbread Man*; lamination supplies or clear contact paper; 6 feet of clothesline; clothespins; a paper star; paper; markers; large resealable bag	
Mighty Minutes 16, "Nothing, Nothing, Something"	Mighty Minutes 25, "Freeze"; dance music	

Day 1 Ministudy

What sounds do we hear at school? Where do they come from?

Vocabulary

English: sounds

Spanish: sonidos

Question of the Day: Do you know what sound this makes? (Show an item from the classroom or school that makes a sound.)

Large Group

Opening Routine

- Sing a welcome song and talk about who's here.

Song: "La La La"

- Use Mighty Minutes 100, "La, La, La." Follow the guidance on the card.

Discussion and Shared Writing: What Are the Sounds We Hear Around School?

- Talk about the question of the day.
- Explain, "I am going to make a sound, and you have to try to figure out what it could be. Listen carefully."
- Stand behind a large piece of cardboard, or a piece of cloth, so children can't see the object you're using. Make a variety of familiar classroom sounds, e.g., a drum beat, keys jingling, shoes walking on the floor, or paper tearing.
- Say, "Those are sounds we hear around our classroom. What are they?"
- Then think aloud, "I wonder what sounds we would hear if we walked around our school."
- Record children's predictions.
- Explain, "Today, we are going to walk around the school and listen for interesting sounds."
- Ask, "What should we do to make sure we can hear very well on our walk? Should we talk quietly and walk softly?"
- Ask, "Where do you think we should walk to hear interesting sounds?" Incorporate children's suggestions into the walk.

> As you walk around the school, stop occasionally and sit together. Invite the children to describe the sounds they hear. Record their ideas. Invite children to close their eyes to help them focus on listening. If possible, make a recording of the sounds they hear.

Before transitioning to interest areas, talk about the variety of containers in the Sand and Water area and how children may use them to make music.

> See Intentional Teaching Card M44, "Musical Water," for more information.

Beginning the Year Ministudy

Choice Time

As you interact with children in the interest areas, make time to

- Occasionally draw children's attention to the sounds in the classroom.

- Use Intentional Teaching Card M44, "Musical Water." Follow the guidance on the card.

Read-Aloud

Read *Rice Is Nice*.

- **Before you read**, show the book cover, and read the title. Ask, "Do you eat rice at home?"
- **As you read**, ask, "How do you eat your rice—with chopsticks, a fork, your fingers, or a spoon?"

- **After you read**, show the picture of the dishes on the last page. Say, "These all look delicious. I wonder what they taste like." Ask, "Have you ever tried rice prepared in one of these ways? What did it taste like?" Tell the children that the book will be available to them on the computer in the Technology area.

Small Group

Option 1: Letters, Letters, Letters

- Use Intentional Teaching Card LL07, "Letters, Letters, Letters." Follow the guidance on the card.

Option 2: Shaving Cream Letters

- Use Intentional Teaching Card LL13, "Shaving Cream Letters." Follow the guidance on the card.

Mighty Minutes®

- Use Mighty Minutes 13, "Simon Says." Follow the guidance on the card.

> While playing "Simon Says," children are practicing what *not* to do. Inhibiting behavior is an important aspect of self-regulation.

Large-Group Roundup

- Recall the day's events.
- Invite children who created music by using water and containers during choice time to share what they discovered.

The Creative Curriculum® for Preschool

Day 2 — Ministudy

What sounds do we hear at school? Where do they come from?

Vocabulary

English: *texture, mystery;* See book Discussion Card 21, *Too Many Tamales* (*¡Qué montón de tamales!*), for additional words.

Spanish: *textura, misterio*

Question of the Day: Which one do you think makes a louder sound? (Display two pictures, e.g., a baby crying and a racing fire engine.)

Large Group

Opening Routine

- Sing a welcome song and talk about who's here.

Game: Listening Story

- Use Mighty Minutes 86, "Listening Story." Follow the guidance on the card.

Discussion and Shared Writing: Choosing Sounds to Investigate

- Talk about the question of the day.
- Recall the sounds the children heard on yesterday's walk.
- Invite children to re-create some of the interesting sounds they heard.
- Ask, "Which of these sounds do we already know about?"
- Discuss their responses, e.g., "Yes, Raymond, I think you're right. That honking sound we heard when we were on the playground was probably a car."
- Say, "Some of the sounds I heard yesterday are a *mystery*. I don't know where they came from or who made them. I wonder what we can do to learn more about them."
- Ask, "Which sounds do we want to find out more about?"
- Record children's ideas.

> The types of sounds in and around your school will depend on your surroundings. Examples of sounds to investigate are those made by the fire alarm, indoor or outdoor machines, crying babies, vehicles screeching to a halt or racing down a street, or people working in the building.

Before transitioning to interest areas, show some of the textured materials that are available in the Discovery area. Explain, "All of these materials have interesting *textures*." Pass them around for children to feel. Ask, "How can we use these materials to create interesting sounds?" Invite children to join you in the Discovery area to experiment with them.

Beginning the Year Ministudy

Choice Time

As you interact with children in the interest areas, make time to

- Ask questions that encourage children to experiment with making sounds, e.g., "What would happen if you rubbed the side of this stick back and forth over this bumpy cardboard?"

> The ability to notice and recognize sounds is called *sound awareness*. Sound awareness is a foundation for phonological awareness, which is the ability to distinguish the small units of sound in spoken language.

Read-Aloud

Read *Too Many Tamales*.

- Use Book Discussion Card 21, *Too Many Tamales*. Follow the guidance for the third read-aloud.

Small Group

Option 1: Letters, Letters, Letters

- Use Intentional Teaching Card LL07, "Letters, Letters, Letters." Follow the guidance on the card.

Option 2: Shaving Cream Letters

- Use Intentional Teaching Card LL13, "Shaving Cream Letters." Follow the guidance on the card.

Mighty Minutes®

- Use Mighty Minutes 76, "Describing Things." Follow the guidance on the card.

Large-Group Roundup

- Recall the day's events.
- Invite children who experimented with sounds in the Discovery area to share what they discovered.

Day 3 Ministudy

What sounds do we hear at school? Where do they come from?

Vocabulary
English: *interview*
Spanish: *entrevista*
Question of the Day: Does this make a sound? (Display a picture of an animal or a familiar item.)

Large Group

Opening Routine
- Sing a welcome song and talk about who's here.

Rhyme: "Here Is the Beehive"
- Use Mighty Minutes 79, "Here Is the Beehive." Follow the guidance on the card.

Discussion and Shared Writing: Investigating Sounds
- Talk about the question of the day.
- Explain, "Today we are going to *interview* someone in our school about one of the sounds we heard on our walk."
- Say, "During the *interview,* we can ask questions about the sound."
- Remind children about the sound. If you recorded it on your walk, play it back for them. Otherwise, describe the sound and where in the school they heard it.
- Ask, "What do we want to ask this person about the sound?"
- Record children's questions and the visitor's responses.

Before transitioning to interest areas, talk about the bells or other musical instruments in the Music and Movement area and how children may use them.

Choice Time

As you interact with children in the interest areas, make time to

- Observe children as they explore the bells or other instruments in the Music and Movement area.
- Ask questions that encourage children to listen closely to the sounds, e.g., "Which bell is the loudest? Does that bell sound higher or lower than this little bell?"

Beginning the Year Ministudy

Read-Aloud

Read *Crazy Pizza Day*.

- **Before you read**, ask, "Why do the people at the pizza shop call this day 'crazy pizza day'?"
- **As you read**, pause to encourage children to fill in missing rhyming words.
- **After you read**, invite children to draw their own crazy pizzas. Record their pizza descriptions, encouraging them to do as much writing themselves as possible. Have children sign their names on their crazy pizza drawings. Create a display of the drawings in the Library area. Tell the children that the book will be available to them on the computer in the Technology area.

Small Group

Option 1: Dinnertime

- Use Intentional Teaching Card M01, "Dinnertime." Follow the guidance on the card.

Option 2: Let's Go Fishing

- Use Intentional Teaching Card M39, "Let's Go Fishing." Follow the guidance on the card.

Mighty Minutes®

- Use Mighty Minutes 02, "Just Like Mine." Follow the guidance on the card.

Large-Group Roundup

- Recall the day's events.
- Lead a conversation about what children learned about the sound discussed during the interview today.

Day 4 Ministudy

What sounds do we hear at school? Where do they come from?

Vocabulary
English: *observe*
Spanish: *observar*
Question of the Day: Does this make a sound? (Display a picture of an animal or a familiar item.)

Large Group

Opening Routine

- Sing a welcome song and talk about who's here.

Song: "La, La, La"

- Use Mighty Minutes 100, "La, La, La." Try the creative version on the back of the card and give each child an instrument to keep the beat.

Discussion and Shared Writing: Investigating Sounds

- Talk about the question of the day.
- Explain, "Today we are going on a site visit to explore further one of the sounds we heard earlier this week."
- If you recorded the sound on your walk, play it back for them. Otherwise, describe the sound and where in the school they heard it.
- Ask, "What else do we want to find out about this sound?" e.g., "What made the sound? Does this sound have a meaning, such as danger, happiness, hunger, or that the machine is working? Does it sound like any other sound we know?"
- Record children's responses.
- Review Intentional Teaching Card LL45, "Observational Drawing." Follow the guidance on the card to have children record information during the site visit.

Before transitioning to interest areas, talk about the headphones in the Technology area and how children may use them to listen to sound clips.

Choice Time

As you interact with children in the interest areas, make time to

- Use descriptive words to talk about sounds you hear during your conversations with children. Use terms such as *loud*, *soft*, *high*, *low*, *screeching*, and *soothing*.

Beginning the Year Ministudy

Read-Aloud

Read *The Gingerbread Man*.

- **Before you read**, ask, "Who remembers the name of this story?"
- **As you read**, pause to encourage children to fill in repetitive text from the story.
- **After you read**, say "The gingerbread man is good at running fast." Ask, "What things are you good at doing?" Tell the children that the book will be available to them on the computer in the Technology area.

Small Group

Option 1: Dramatic Story Retelling

- Use Intentional Teaching Card LL06, "Dramatic Story Retelling." Follow the guidance on the card using *The Gingerbread Man*.

> See *Volume 3: Literacy*, Chapter 3 for more information on retelling stories.

Option 2: Clothesline Storytelling

- Use Intentional Teaching Card LL33, "Clothesline Storytelling." Follow the guidance on the card using *The Gingerbread Man*.

Mighty Minutes®

- Use Mighty Minutes 16, "Nothing, Nothing, Something." Follow the guidance on the card.

Large-Group Roundup

- Recall the day's events.
- Invite children to share their observational drawings with the group.
- Discuss what the group can learn from each recorded observation.
- Remind children that some of the sounds at school give us important information, such as the fire alarm or the cleanup song.

Day 5 Ministudy

What sounds do we hear at school? Where do they come from?

Vocabulary

English: *remember*

Spanish: *recordar*

Question of the Day: Can we make sounds with this? (Display an empty container.)

Large Group

Opening Routine

- Sing a welcome song and talk about who's here.

Music: "Echo Clapping"

- Use Mighty Minutes 26, "Echo Clapping." Try the "pattern" version on the back of the card using drums or rhythm sticks.

Discussion and Shared Writing: Celebrating Our Learning

- Review the information that children gathered from their investigation of school sounds.
- Invite children to recall some of the sounds they heard on their walk around the school. Ask, "What sounds do you *remember* from our walk around the school?"
- Talk about the question of the day.
- Provide a collection of empty containers and other interesting classroom objects that can produce sound. Ask, "How can we use these as instruments to make our own interesting sounds?"
- Invite children to explore the materials in different ways to create a variety of sounds. Then have children play their "instruments" and sing familiar tunes together.

Before transitioning to interest areas, explain that these new instruments will be in the Music and Movement area.

Choice Time

As you interact with children in the interest areas, make time to

- Help children interpret the emotions of others, e.g., say, "Look at that smile on Lucy's face. That means she's happy that you shared the drum with her."

Beginning the Year Ministudy

Read-Aloud

Read *A World of Families*.

- **Before you read**, remind children that this book is about things that different families do together.
- **As you read**, compare what the families do in the book to things the children do together at school.
- **After you read**, draw a simple Venn diagram with two overlapping circles. Label one circle, "Things we do with our families"; label the middle, "Things we do in both places"; and label the other circle, "Things we do at school." Review the ideas in the book and ask, "Is this something we do at school, too, or something that we do only with our families?" Record each idea in the proper place on the Venn diagram. Tell the children that the book will be available to them on the computer in the Technology area.

A Venn diagram is a drawing that shows relationships among sets. The diagram often has two or more intersecting circles. The shaded area where the circles overlap shows elements that the sets have in common.

Small Group

- **Option 1: Dramatic Story Retelling**
- Use Intentional Teaching Card LL06, "Dramatic Story Retelling." Follow the guidance on the card using *The Gingerbread Man*.

- **Option 2: Clothesline Storytelling**
- Use Intentional Teaching Card LL33, "Clothesline Storytelling." Follow the guidance on the card using *The Gingerbread Man*.

Mighty Minutes®

- Use Mighty Minutes 25, "Freeze." Follow the guidance on the card.

Large-Group Roundup

- Recall the day's events.
- Invite children to share something they enjoyed doing during choice time.

The Creative Curriculum® for Preschool

Resources

Integrating Mathematics Throughout the Day

> For more information on integrating mathematics throughout the day, see *The Creative Curriculum for Preschool, Volume 4, Mathematics.*

Arrival

Preparing the Environment
- Create an attendance chart, e.g., *Who's at School? Who's at Home?*.
- Post written procedures for routines, e.g., washing hands, toileting. Use numerals to indicate what to do first, second, third, etc.
- Post instructions for class jobs that show math used in meaningful ways, e.g., *Feed Cottontail 1 handful of hay, ½ cup pellets, 2 carrots, and 1 bowl of water.*

Interactions
- Have informal conversations that facilitate mathematics learning and thinking, e.g., "Your shirt has an interesting pattern. Can you read it?"
- Talk with children about routine procedures and what they do first, second, third.

Large-Group Time

Preparing the Environment
- Refer to the attendance chart.
- Post a math-related "Question of the Day" or "Problem of the Week."
- Post a picture/word daily schedule.
- Post a weekly or monthly class calendar to document and call attention to meaningful events or special days.
- Prepare materials, including visuals (e.g., manipulatives, books and related props, charts, posters, pictures, tapes/CDs, or flannel board cutouts) for any math concepts you want to introduce.
- Use puppets or props with rhymes and songs.

Interactions
- Refer to the schedule throughout the day. Talk about what the children will do *after* the group meeting, *before* lunch, etc. Use words, such as *morning* and *afternoon*, as well as *first*, *next*, and *last*. Discuss the plans for *today*. Review some things that the group did *yesterday*. Use a clothespin to indicate the current time of the day and have a child move it appropriately during the day.
- Call attention to upcoming events or special days recorded on the class calendar. Discuss things that happened *yesterday* or might happen *today* or *tomorrow*. Record them on the calendar.

Choice Time

Preparing the Environment
- Create choice boards for interest areas that indicate the number of children who may be in a given area at a time.

- Organize materials in ways that encourage children to sort and classify.
- Equip all interest areas with mathematics materials.
- Add math-related books appropriate to each interest area.
- Add writing, drawing, and construction materials so children can represent their discoveries and learning.
- Post step-by-step instructions for using equipment, e.g., computers, or handling routine tasks, e.g., cleaning up an area.
- Add timers so children can learn about and manage their time in a favorite interest area or with a toy or game.

Interactions
- Talk about the number of children an area can accommodate. Discuss how to figure out whether there is room for others.
- Model and "think aloud" about how you are using a new material, your approach to solving a problem, or ways to collect and report data.

Small-Group Time

Preparing the Environment
- Prepare print or visual materials, e.g., recipes, song charts, and rhymes.
- Add props, flannel materials, and storyboards for storytelling or retelling.
- Prepare materials and supplies, such as manipulatives, tapes/CDs, games, or writing materials to conduct a focused activity.

Interactions
- Play mathematical games indoors and outdoors.
- Offer sorting and graphing experiences.

Snack and Mealtime

Preparing the Environment
- Post step-by-step instructions for routines, e.g., washing hands. Use numerals to indicate what to do first, second, third, etc.
- Include snack and/or lunch helpers on the job chart, e.g. to set the table and pass out supplies.
- Post self-serve snack charts and picture/word recipes.
- Include cups, spoons, and other containers in a variety of sizes for children to learn about measurement, quantity, and capacity.

Snack and Mealtime, continued

Interactions
- Read the self-serve snack charts and recipes. Assist children with counting, measuring, and following the appropriate steps in the preparation process. Use open-ended questions and comments as you interact.
- Call attention to shapes, sizes, categories, and patterns of foods, e.g., "An orange is like a ball, Dallas. Another name for its shape is *sphere*…"; "Look at the pattern on the rind of this watermelon. Let's read it…"; "This piece of felt is a large triangle. Can you name the shapes of other felt pieces in this box?"

Transitions

Preparing the Environment
- Think in advance about appropriate mathematical songs, rhymes, chants, or games to use.
- Prepare materials you need for the activity, e.g., numeral cards, geometric shapes.

Interactions
- Measurement, e.g., "Make yourself as short [tall] as you can when you walk to the sink."
- Sorting, e.g., "If you're wearing something green, go with Mr. Alvarez for story time."

Outdoor Time

Preparing the Environment
- Provide measuring tools, e.g., cups for the Sand and Water area; string or rulers for plants.
- Provide equipment, such as tunnels, traffic cones, balls, boxes.
- Provide writing materials for children to use to record mathematical information.

Interactions
- Use math vocabulary as you talk about ways in which children move and play.
- Encourage children to look at and draw objects from a variety of perspectives.

Rest Time

Preparing the Environment
- Establish a rest-time routine.
- Play music that has a slow rhythm.
- Display a clock.

Interactions
- Remind children of the routines and patterns of rest time, e.g., prepare their mats, get blankets, and use the restroom.
- Offer quiet activities with a mathematical focus to children who do not nap, e.g., stringing attribute beads, working with pattern blocks.

Departure
Preparing the Environment
- Review the daily schedule and the calendar of events.
- Prepare mathematical materials for children to take home and share with their families.

Interactions
- Review important events about which children want to tell family members.
- Call attention to what the clock looks like when it is time to go home.

Beginning the Year Resources

Integrating Literacy Throughout the Day

For more information on integrating literacy throughout the day, see *The Creative Curriculum for Preschool, Volume 3: Literacy.*

Arrival

Preparing the Environment
- Create an attendance chart and a name card for each child.
- Have children and parents sign in each day.
- Create job and helper charts. Post any directions children might need for completing a job, e.g., how to care for the class pet.
- Post a "Question of the Day" and provide supplies for children to respond in writing.
- Create a message board for children and families to send and receive notes.

Interactions
- Have informal conversations with children and family members.
- Interact with children to facilitate language learning, e.g., talk with children, ask open-ended questions, play with children, and model literate behavior.

Large-Group Time

Preparing the Environment
- Display a daily schedule that is presented with pictures and words, and refer to it throughout the day.
- Display a chart with words to the song, story, or rhyme you are using.
- Prepare name cards to use during group activities.
- Have books and related props ready for story time.
- Have blank chart paper and markers ready for interactive writing.

Interactions
- Have children share news about important events and experiences in their lives.
- Introduce new vocabulary as you present new props, materials, and activities.

Choice time

Preparing the Environment
- Create choice boards for interest areas. Have children's name cards ready so they can use them to indicate their decisions.
- Provide literacy props for children's play.
- Provide abundant writing materials for children to document their learning and discoveries.
- Create sign-up sheets for favorite activities.
- Display intriguing pictures in interest areas to encourage conversation and writing.

- Write and post rules or directions for using particular materials and equipment. Review them with the children when necessary.
- Post picture and word directions for routine procedures, e.g., washing hands, and call attention to them.

Interactions
- Talk and sing with children; ask open-ended questions; play with children; retell stories; model reading and writing; and call attention to letters, words, and other features of print.
- Call attention to signs, labels, and other print in various interest areas. Talk about the functions of each. Involve children in creating new signs or labels for the areas throughout the year.

Small-Group Time

Preparing the Environment
- Prepare print materials for various activities, such as recipe charts, poems, name cards, and blank books.
- Keep blank chart paper and markers ready for recording children's ideas.
- Have books and props ready for reading aloud, storytelling, and retelling.

Interactions
- Write with the children, e.g., charts, letters to people, or lists.
- Invite children to bring and read environmental print from home.

Snack and Mealtime

Preparing the Environment
- Write, review, and post the breakfast, lunch, and snack menus.
- Post written procedures for washing hands and cleaning dishes.
- Post the picture and word recipe if children are to make their own snacks.
- Label the food items that the children will use to prepare their snacks.

Interactions
- Read the recipes and ingredient labels with the children.
- Have informal conversations with children.

Transitions

Preparing the Environment
- Prepare name cards to use when dismissing children to interest areas.
- Think about appropriate songs, rhymes, and chants in advance.

Transitions, continued

Interactions
- Play a variety of language games.
- Sing and recite rhymes, chants, or fingerplays, both to signal the beginning of a transition and to facilitate learning while children are waiting.

Outdoor Time

Preparing the Environment
- Create inviting areas for reading and writing.
- Provide materials for children to record their outdoor discoveries.
- Provide materials for labeling plants.
- Incorporate signs that the children might see elsewhere in the community, e.g., road signs, exit signs, and warning signs.

Interactions
- Have informal conversations with children.
- Sing and recite rhymes or chants, e.g., while children are jumping rope or playing hand games.

Rest Time

Preparing the Environment
- Offer books and writing materials, e.g., magic slates, magnetic drawing boards, and chalkboards, for children who do not sleep.
- Play soft music or recordings of environmental sounds, e.g., ocean, wind, and night sounds.

Interactions
- Read a soothing story in a calm tone before the children rest.

Departure

Preparing the Environment
- Prepare literacy packs for children to take home and share with their families.
- Record "What We Did Today" on an erasable board or a chart outside of the classroom so family members can discuss the day's events with their child.

Interactions
- Talk about the events of the day. Record the highlights on the class calendar, a chart, or in a class journal.
- Say something special to each child as you say good-bye.

Children's Books

In addition to the children's books specifically used in this *Teaching Guide*, you may wish to supplement daily activities and interest areas with some of the following children's books.

Abuelita Full of Life/Llena de vida (Amy Costales)

All Families Are Special (Norma Simon)

Amelia's Road (Linda Jacobs Altman)

And Tango Makes Three (Peter Parnell)

Be My Neighbor (Maya Ajmera and John D. Ivanko)

black is brown is tan (Arnold Adoff)

Black, White, Just Right! (Marguerite Davol)

Butterfly Boy (Virginia Kroll)

Chicken Sunday (Patricia Polacco)

Chrysanthemum (Kevin Henkes)

Cleversticks (Bernard Ashley)

Dear Juno (Soyung Pak)

Elizabeti's School (Stephanie Stuve-Bodeen)

Elizabeti's Doll (Stephanie Stuve-Bodeen)

The Empanadas That Abuela Made/Las empanadas que hacía la abuela (Diane Gonzales Bertrand)

Everything Is Different at Nonna's House (Caron Lee Cohen)

Families (Ann Morris)

The Family Book (Todd Parr)

Family, Familia (Diane González Bertrand)

Family Pictures/Cuadros de familia (Carmen Lomas Garza)

From Father to Son (Patricia Almada)

First Day (Dandi Daley Mackall)

First Day Jitters (Julie Danneberg)

First Experiences: My First Day at Preschool (Roger Priddy)

Friends at School (Rochelle Bunnett)

Froggy Goes to School (Jonathan London)

Gracias, The Thanksgiving Turkey (Joy Cowley)

Grandma and Me at the Flea/Los meros meros remateros (Juan Felipe Herrera)

The Hello, Goodbye Window (Norton Juster)

Hurray for Pre-K! (Ellen Senisi)

I Am Not Going to School Today! (Robie Harris)

I Love Saturdays y domingos (Alma Flor Ada)

Icy Watermelon / Sandia fría (Patricia Almada)

In My Family / En mi familia (Carmen Lomas Garza)

Isla (Arthur Dorros)

Jonathan and His Mommy (Irene Smalls)

Julius, The Baby of the World (Kevin Henkes)

Liliana's Grandmothers / Las abuelas de Liliana (Leyla Torres)

Llama Llama Misses Mama (Anna Dewdney)

Loving (Ann Morris)

Children's Books, continued

Mama, Do You Love Me? (Barbara Joosse)

Minerva Louise at School (Janet Morgan Stoeke)

Moony Luna / Luna, Lunita Lunera (Jorge Argueta)

A Mother for Chaco (Keiko Kasza)

Mouse's First Day of School (Lauren Thompson)

Mrs. Katz and Tush (Patricia Polacco)

My Hippie Grandmother (Reeve Lindbergh)

My Nana and Me (Irene Smalls)

My Pop Pop and Me (Irene Smalls)

My Tata's Guitar (Ethriam Cash Brammer)

Nana Upstairs, Nana Downstairs (Tomie dePaola)

Neighborhood Walk: Small Town (Peggy Pancella)

Night Shift Daddy (Eileen Spinelli)

Now One Foot, Now the Other (Tomie DePaola)

On Mother's Lap (Ann Herbert Scott)

Papa, Do You Love Me? (Barbara Joosse)

A Place to Grow (Soyung Pak)

Quinito's Neighborhood/El vecindario de Quinito (José Ramírez)

The Relatives Came (Cynthia Rylant)

Shoes From Grandpa (Mem Fox)

Sitti's Secrets (Naomi Shihab Nye)

Starting School (Allan Ahlberg)

Sumi's First Day of School (Joung Um Kim)

Timothy Goes to School (Rosemary Wells)

Two Homes (Claire Masurel)

We Are Cousins / Somos primos (Diane Gonzales Bertrand)

We Had a Picnic This Sunday Past (Jacqueline Woodson)

When I Am Old With You (Angela Johnson)

The White Swan Express (Jean Davies Okimoto)

Who's in a Family? (Robert Skutch)

Will I Have a Friend? (Miriam Cohen)

Xóchitl and the Flowers/Xóchitl, la niña de las flores (Jorge Argueta)

Teacher Resources

The teacher resources provide additional information and ideas for establishing and maintaining a high-quality preschool program.

Beyond Behavior Management: The Six Life Skills Children Need in Today's World (Jenna Bilmes)

Building Blocks for Teaching Preschoolers With Special Needs, 2nd Edition (Susan R. Sandall, Ilene S. Schwartz)

Children's Play: The Roots of Reading (Edward Zigler, Dorothy G. Singer, Sandra J. Bishop-Josef, Editors)

Designs for Living and Learning: Transforming Early Childhood Environments (Deb Curtis, Margie Carter)

Developmentally Appropriate Practice in Early Childhood Programs Serving Children From Birth Through Age 8, Third Edition (Carol Copple, Sue Bredekamp, Editors)

From Parents to Partners: Building a Family-Centered Early Childhood Program (Janis Keyser)

One Child, Two Languages: A Guide for Early Childhood Educators of Children Learning English as a Second Language, 2nd Edition (Patton O. Tabors)

Weekly Planning Form

Week of: _____ Teacher: _____ Study: _____

	Monday	Tuesday	Wednesday	Thursday	Friday
Interest Areas					
Large Group					
Read-Aloud					
Small Group					

Outdoor Experiences:

Family Partnerships:

Wow! Experiences:

Beginning the Year Resources

Weekly Planning Form, continued

"To Do" List:

Reflecting on the week:

Individual Child Planning

The Creative Curriculum® for Preschool